BLOOD, MARRIAGE, WINE  glitter

essays by S. Bear Bergman

D0047424

ARSENAL PULP PRESS ✦ VANCOUVER

ARSENAL PULP PRESS
Suite 202 – 211 East Georgia St.
Vancouver, BC V6A 1Z6
Canada
arsenalpulp.com

The publisher gratefully acknowledges the support of the Canada Council for the Arts and the British Columbia Arts Council for its publishing program, and the Government of Canada (through the Canada Book Fund) and the Government of British Columbia (through the Book Publishing Tax Credit Program) for its publishing activities.

Excerpt from "We Who Are Your Closest Friends" by Phillip Lopate from *At the End of the Day: Selected Poems and an Introductory Essay* (Marsh Hawk Press, 2009). Reprinted with permission of the author.

"What They See" first appeared in *The Rumpus,* at *therumpus.com.*
"Brother Dog" first appeared in *Persistence: All Ways Butch and Femme,* edited by Ivan E. Coyote and Zena Sharman (Arsenal Pulp Press, 2011).
"Hiddur Mitvah" will also appear in *A Family By Any Other Name: Exploring Queer Relationships,* edited by Bruce Gillespie (TouchWood Editions Ltd., 2014).

Editing by Susan Safyan
Book design by Gerilee McBride

Printed and bound in Canada

Library and Archives Canada Cataloguing in Publication

Bergman, S. Bear, 1974-
[Essays. Selections]
     Blood, marriage, wine & glitter / S. Bear Bergman.

Issued in print and electronic formats.
ISBN 978-1-55152-511-2 (pbk.).—ISBN 978-1-55152-512-9 (epub)

     1. Gay parents. 2. Families. 3. Gender identity.
4. Transsexuals—Identity. 5. Sex (Psychology). I. Title.

HQ75.27.B47 2013   306.874086'64   C2013-903247-9

                                                        C2013-903248-7

For Bobby, Hanne, Kate, Turner & Zev,
who chose me and let me choose them.

Contents

Acknowledgments

First and foremost, breaking the tradition of saving the most important or most significant thank-you for last, I have to lavish my gratitude on my beloved husband Ishai. Think of it like when the Oscar-winning actor gets his name above the title on the poster; there's really just absolutely no way in the world this gets done without him—not this book, not our amazing kid, not my well and happy life, none of it. He's got such a big brain and such a big heart (not to mention an exceptionally nice backside) and he pitched in so many extra hours of household chores and took dozens of extra nights of kid-bedtime duty and provided innumerable pep-talks—all so I could get to the part where I actually sit and write. Thank you, Mister Husband. You're a true Badger of Honour.

Stanley, someday you will be old enough to read this acknowledgment. Thank you, Monkeyboy Lovechop, for all the gummy sharks and snuggles and sweet kisses, for doing all sorts of very wise or very cute things, and for being patient with your Papa when he couldn't play. Thanks also to Levi Jane, who remains a Very Good Dog.

My chosen family and wonderful friends were all in this with me as usual, asking questions and telling stories and prompting ideas and keeping me as close to reasonably sane as I get, as well as helping to entertain Stanley in the home stretch and being just generally as awesome as a million hot dogs. For all of these things and more as well as just plain being fan-damn-tastic, I thank Calvin Anderson, Laura Antoniou, Toni Amato, Dr John Austin, Morgan Baskin, Joseph Berman, Judy and Steve Berman, Hanne Blank, Kate Bornstein, Ivan Coyote, Dr Leigh Ann Craig, Marian Fulton, Katie Herzig, T. Aaron Hans, Laura Waters Jackson, Kate Larkin, Dr Robert Lawrence, Zev Lowe, Seth Marnin, Bobby Peck, Tori Paulman, Dr Carol Queen, Rabbi Danya Ruttenberg, Abi Salole, Scott Turner Schofield, Dr Zena Sharman, Karen Taylor, and Chris Veldhoven as well as the Stevens/Shapiro family, the Ware/ Redman family, the Fairley/Andersen family, the Berdichevsky/ Sereaki family, the super-fabulous folks of PQLF and the House of Consent.

Thanks also to my family of origin for all their support, my parents Carlyn and Michael Bergman, my uncles David Bergman & John Lessner, my grandma Rita Bergman, and my Nana, Barbara Baker. Special gratitude as ever to my brother Jeffrey Bergman and sister-in-law Lisa Bergman, plus my two high-quality nephews, their boys Levi and Samuel. Great thanks also to my in-laws, David and Diane Wallace, and my sister-in-law Bronwen Wallace.

I would be remiss if I didn't thank a few other people whose various specialties provided so much assistance: all the lovely folks at Arsenal Pulp Press, Angel Adeyoha, Deborah Frolick, Paul Petrie, Juli Rivera, Danielle Sutherland, Anne Wilson, and Rhea Wilson. A loving and also uncompromising cadre of trans women made me stop using the t-word (which you will not find in my books or out of my mouth anymore) through personal intervention or through their work, and my debt of gratitude is to Ryka Aoki, Danielle Askini, Julie Blair, Red Durkin, Andrea Jenkins, and extra much to Alexandra Rodriguez De Ruiz along with my sincerest apologies for how long it took me to come correct on that point. I'm also grateful for the work of Leslie Feinberg, Anne Lamott, Julian F. Thompson, Stephen Sondheim, and Aaron Sorkin as I thought and wrote.

Last, thank you to all the wonderful audiences I've had since the last book, who have asked me so sweetly when the words they heard on an evening of storytelling might be available to them in book form. Here you go. Thanks again.

The Really True Story, Once and for All, of How We Got Stanley (with Footnotes)[1]

It's not uncommon, as a pair of queer trans things, that Ishai and I are asked where Stanley came from. I used to say "the stork brought him," and now I typically say—in a voice full of laughter—"Well. When two transsexuals love each other very, *very* much, they give each other a special hug ... "[2] Then I wait for the laugh. Sometimes instead I get the bewildered grin, or maybe the shudder of disgust, but mostly people have the good manners to at least give me a grin for the sheer absurdity of it all.

I teach a workshop called Is It Okay To Ask My Question? about how our own locations of cultural privilege[3] and disempowerment[4] shape our sense of entitlement to ask other people personal

---

1 I know, I'm not typically a footnote-y guy. I'm sorry if you're reading this on an older e-reader. But footnotes really are the best way to include all manner of specifics, and my experience on this topic is that I will get asked questions about the specifics until I want to give up my career and hide under the bed, so it seems just as well to answer it all—every bit of it—once and then refer people to this book ever after.

2 This is a very common way of describing to young children how they were made.

3 Where our race, class, gender expression, sexuality, ability status, religion, or similar gives us unasked-for benefits in society.

4 The opposite of privilege, where one or more of those same things produces undeserved suppression of our interests.

questions. In it, I make the point that one of the things we need to be aware of, when we are in a privileged location, is that one of the ways disempowerment works is that the very information a privileged person wants ("Do you wash your dreadlocks?" "Oh, so Chanukah is your Christmas?" "Wait, so can you get married?" and so on) is erased from the cultural landscape. The fact that they don't already know it is a function of their privilege: the mainstream media only reflects people and experiences that are substantially like their own. It's interesting to watch this lesson settle in when I ask whether they have ever seen a model with dreadlocks in a shampoo commercial, or a sitcom family settling in for iftar,[5] or an episode of *Baby Stories* about a family in which one or both partners are transsexual.

So when I say, "Well. When two transsexuals love each other very, *very* much, they give each other a special hug ..." and then just trail off, I'm relying on that same thing. I'm hoping people will grasp that while I do not think there is anything shameful in the details, I am not always interested in sharing them upon command with someone I don't know.

I have come to understand, however, that there are some problems with this choice. Not the least of which is that it does not stop people from pausing a moment to appreciate my sense of humour and then—after a brief courtesy ha-ha—asking me again in a slightly more interrogatory tone, "No, but really. How?" And whatever kind of somewhat vague answer I might offer, once I open the door to the question, people press me more and more to reveal every possible detail until they feel satisfied that they

---

5   The meal after fasting during Ramadan.

know every single, possible thing about *how*. Exactly, specifically, no-detail-left-behind how.

Okay, fine. I'll tell you how:

Ishai and I started talking about children almost immediately. I tend to joke that pretty much the first conversation we ever had with our clothes on was about children. He was, at the time, actively pursuing parenting and wanted me to know that—if I had any intention to be in his world in any serious way. I was not at all sure that I wanted kids, but I said I was willing to sit with it and see how it felt as time passed.[6]

Time passed. Ishai's babymaking desires started to be even more present for us. I wanted a slow-down—I wanted to enjoy a few years of being carefree, childless people before we started a life of dirty diapers and muddy socks and scale models of the Parthenon made out of sugar cubes and so on. Ishai felt equally strongly that we could be child-at-home-less and carefree in our fifties, when we would enjoy it more, and that we should get started making a baby now, right that minute. Which, without a great deal more ado, we did.

Ultimately, we chose a known donor, a lovely rabbinical student (now a rabbi) with whom Ishai had been roommates some years before at a gathering of the National Havurah Summer Institute. I'd never met him, but I weirdly wasn't that concerned about it, especially because it offered me an opportunity to take a break from frantically scouring catalogues of donor sperm, looking for The Perfect Donor. I was becoming uncomfortable with the

---

6 Yes, indeed, this was an early stage of a relationship to be discussing children. But we both knew that we had made a very powerful connection, and we were laying our cards on the table, as it were. I also made a list of all my faults, and sent it to him. (He concurs that this was a surprisingly romantic gesture—It's not just me).

eugenics experiment in which I suddenly found myself, looking for the tallest man with the largest number of advanced degrees and spoken languages,[7] wrestling with whether it seemed important that the donor be Jewish, and so on. It was also beginning to dawn on me that perhaps we were just selecting for someone who was very good at filling in forms. The idea that we'd use the sperm of a real person allowed me to focus on the actual qualities in a person that I truly value: intelligence and kindness.[8]

Jacob turned out to be smart and kind. And, after a period of reflection, interested in helping us to spawn. We had several sweet and earnest meetings all together in which we wrote up a document of our intentions and responsibilities. My memories of this are the outdoor table in the garden of our first apartment together, a basement suite that leaked in any meteorological condition except blazing sunshine but had a remarkable outdoor space. We took turns making notes while we ate and drank and talked and talked, cozy in the garden surrounded by the flowers of the bolted lettuce. As a way to make room for a new small person in the world, it was really beautiful—tender and close and full of loving intention. We also did a "dry run" of what insemination might look like, without doing anything much with the sperm, just so we wouldn't be losing time figuring out the mechanics of who went where to do what while the baby juice was losing motility by the second. I recommend both of these experiences to any prospective parent, though heterosexuals would require specific circumstances to implement the latter portion.

---

7 The neuroscientist who reported that he spoke four languages fluently was five-foot-five and a Jehovah's Witness. ::sigh::

8 Okay, also tall.

By late winter, we were ready to go. Ishai and I were to be married in May, and—

Oh, wait. Right. My husband was going to be the one getting pregnant. This has been a fact of my life for so long that I forget it's even a thing, but it is. Mister Wonderful, with particular emphasis on both parts of that nickname, was planning to get knocked up. Trans guys can get pregnant under some bodily circumstances and they have been doing it for far longer than Thomas Beatie's publicity machine would have you believe. We'd done a variety of fertility-related gymkhana in advance of this, including making ourselves an appointment at our suburban fertility clinic (the only one in town) and bringing our reproductive endocrinologist up to speed on transmasculine fertility, reproduction, and birth with friendly smiles and steely resolve. They didn't kick us out, so we had a fertility specialist. Carrying on.

—we were kind of hoping for a shotgun wedding. We had two chances to make this dream come true. We turned out to be in San Francisco for chance number one. Although it was somewhat last-minute, we asked an old friend of mine (recently the father of gorgeous twins) if he might be willing to sign on for a one-shot deal, as it were. No one was especially surprised when it didn't take, but Ishai was happy to be actively, actually *trying* and I was just happy. Everyone was happy.

The next month, in April, the plan had been that we were going to visit my folks for Pesach[9] and then on to Boston for another go at babymaking. However, my gallbladder exploded, nixing the trip, which ultimately turned out to be for the best—the timing

---

9   A Jewish holiday commemorating the redemption of the Jews from slavery in Egypt.

was off.[10] The right time for a try was actually two weeks later, by which time I was supposed to be in Nashville for work and Ishai was scheduled to be in Buffalo for a weekend with a friend and playmate.[11] She's a flight attendant, and so would occasionally accept a route with a highly undesirable layover, in this case: arrive in Buffalo late Saturday night, stay all Sunday in Buffalo, and leave at sparrowfart-o'clock[12] on Monday. It gave them a whole day together and a company-provided hotel room in which to spend it.

Well, says I, maybe Jacob would be willing to go to Buffalo for the weekend too?

You might think it would be a little weird, spending the weekend in two adjacent hotel rooms in Buffalo with a person you're sharing bodily fluids with but not having sex with,[13] and a person you're having sex with but not sharing bodily fluids with. Ishai reports that it was, in fact, lovely; that he felt completely relaxed and very much loved and cared for (given that I was in Nashville at the time). I wanted to be there, but we had reached a point of onward we go, so I sent sparkly, spawning thoughts northward and did my gigs in Nashville. I felt glad and excited that Ishai was in such a tender place, with friends and loved ones. Monica, the flight attendant in question, is a santera[14] and the combined

---

10   It had seemed right when we made the plan and bought plane tickets in January, but by April we were out of whack.

11   Yes, that is a euphemism.

12   Anything earlier than six a.m.

13   They used a sterile plastic bottle and a syringe with a flexible tube instead of a needle.

14   A priestess in the religion of Santería.

intercessions of the santera and the rabbi evidently worked: Ishai got pregnant on the first go.

Strangely, I felt almost sure this would be so. I'd told him from the beginning that I thought he would get pregnant on the first try, while he insisted that it would take months, maybe a year. Our timelines to baby were firmly predicated on our predictions of babymaking success: I was unshakable in my belief that it would take the first time (which it pretty much did, except for the somewhat ceremonial San Francisco attempt), and Ishai figured it would take forever. It didn't. When he arrived to collect me from the airport four days after this Buffalo business, I knew for certain, though don't ask me how. In some unknowable way, however, I could already feel Stanley coming into being. The air around Ishai was charged. I knew we were already on the ride.

Six weeks later, on May 24, we got married. We told only a few people that Ishai was pregnant—his best friend, my brother, our parents (and then, when we couldn't contain ourselves anymore, our wonderful wedding party). All day I leaned into him and murmured in his ear, "Hi, baby," and he'd just smile and smile. I confess to initiating hundreds of small retail transactions during those next five weeks, before the first trimester had finished and we—by mutual agreement—could tell people our good news, all for the pleasure of replying to a clerk's "How are you today, sir?" with "I'm going to be a Dad! How are *you*?"

Strangely, nobody ever rolled an eye at me for this behaviour.

And that, as they say, is that. The story is either boring or extraordinary, depending on the lens through which you regard it. With the assistance of some truly spectacular midwives (and a hospital staff who had been well prepped by them ahead of time),

Ishai gave birth at forty-one weeks and six days[15] to a giant baby with a full head of hair and the most exceptional face I have ever, ever seen. We named him Stanley, as we had planned to all along. Everyone was healthy and well. I took hundreds of photos of him, of them both, and my parents, Ishai's parents, and Jacob's parents all said he looked *just* like we had, when we were brand new. Eventually, by evening, we all collapsed to sleep, overwhelmed by our big days.

The rest is as commonplace and exceptional as baby stories always are—you arrive to the birth as two people and you leave as three.[16] Up until that point, even our somewhat unusual story is just a story. Then we went home. That's where the real adventure begins.

---

15   a.k.a. Really Late. They were starting to talk about monitoring the amniotic fluid and all sorts of other things when Stanley finally decided to be ready.

16   Or more.

Starting a Family

"When did you decide to start a family?" she asks, and then amends the question. "How, I mean, I guess. How did you decide ... what was your decision-making model? If that's not too personal a question?"

At the moment of this serious query, I am on a panel at the 519 Church Street Community Centre in Toronto, sitting in front of a class of expectant parents. Typically they are split into Dykes Planning Tykes and Daddies & Papas To Be, but for this event the groups combine into one to hear from all sorts of parenting queers and transpeeps. I am a regular panellist at these events because the Parenting Coordinator here (Chris Veldhoven in his professional life) is my son's Sparkle Chris, and said son—Stanley—is his Sparkling. Thus I am obligated by family ties to come and talk about family ties, a situation I relish in theory even though it's a little inconvenient in practice.

The question makes me laugh inside. I understand that in Straightpeoplelandia, "starting a family" is what they call it when you spawn, which I surely have done. But the actual answer to this question is a) that family found me, b) that I was fifteen at the time, and c) my "decision-making model" appeared in the glittery form of a nineteen-year-old drag queen who settled herself in on my lap during a Boston Alliance of Gay and Lesbian Youth (fondly known as BAGLY) meeting in 1991. When she snuggled herself slightly against me, I instinctively put an arm around her for warmth and comfort. It seemed like a small enough act, but it prompted her to dub me "baby big brother." In that moment, and in the queerest possible sense, I found myself in the family way. Ever since, I've been working to stay that way.

So, of course, I know what my lesbian interlocutor means. I'm assured by Chris that I answered her question kindly and coherently. But in my storytelling mind I was already spinning down a long road of thoughtfulness about what it means to start a family, or make a family, and how it works. How the families of my youth—friends and peers put together by time and circumstance and bonded by love and desire and pure raw neediness—have mostly faded away. I would have told you for sure that I would always, absolutely, be close with the people in question—that I could imagine being eighty and zipping Jasmine (which is a pseudonym but captures the spirit of her chosen name) into her drags (as she called the dresses in which she performed), she who called me first Mama Bear and then Poppa Bear, taught me how to zip without catching any hair or skin in the zipper no matter how tight the garment, and showed me how to twist and oil her dreadlocks so she could stay flawless.

If you're straight, it might be difficult to understand how these groups of friends became families, so surely and distinctly. All I can tell you is that Maslow's hierarchy of needs is real, and the feeling of belonging gains a special lustre when you're without it for quite some time. Many of us come out into long, howling silences; some come out into war zones, our chairs at the kitchen table becoming ejector seats. True, plenty of us homos and gender-benders eventually manage to have some kind of reasonable relationships with our parents, but some of them are tenuous or conditional peaces at best. Beyond that, most of our parents are straight. Our fathers have never longed to kiss a boy, and our mothers might not be ready to talk about it with their sons. Our parents might not be ready to teach us how to tie a necktie, or put on liquid eyeliner, or shop for the clothes that affirm our genders or signal our interest to people we find appealing, or any of the other mysteries and complexities we need to puzzle out as young people. It's surprising how many there are, and equally surprising how gendered they can be—a fact we don't really notice until all parties are on the far side of the experience, which I mention to those of you who say, "But I would have taught my kid those things, if ze'd asked!"

We establish for ourselves cells of belonging, where we can feel fully known and accepted and also mentored and able to mentor others. Families. Often without a decision-making model to be found anywhere.

Though Jas could have been a model, if she'd lived long enough.

(I don't actually know what happened to her or whether she's for-sure dead. She stopped coming to BAGLY. I saw her once more that year—1991—at Pride, and she told me she'd tested positive for HIV. She did not look at all well, and was wearing pants for the first time since I'd met her—baggy jeans, with a missing belt loop. I never saw her again, and I heard that she'd moved home to Leominster or someplace and died. If you're alive, babygirl, if this has somehow come into your hands: please call me. Among other things, I have some photos you will not *believe*.)

At seventeen, and even still a decade later at twenty-seven, I was in love with the *idea* of family in a way that was uncomplicated and uncritical. I valued it in a complicated way, made out of both an intense sense of belonging to my larger family (the Bergman/ Fergensen side, especially deeply) and also really not belonging

23

to, or feeling much wanted within, my nuclear family unit. Not as I was, anyhow; not if I was going to carry on being queer and butch and far too mouthy about both of those identities for my own good (also known as "for my relatives' comfort"). I think many people are in love with the idea of family; lots of us have long and complex fantasies about it from the time we're small.

Even for those of us who have had delightful coming-out experiences and perfectly lovely relationships with our families of origin, though, it remains true that for many of us queer people the traditional avenues to Starting A Family have been closed to us. Marriage has been a contested situation for most of us for the majority of time we've been out, depending on where we live (and even if we live somewhere with legal and widely accepted gay marriage, it's still complicated by our community history and ideals). Childmaking, ditto, is a newly available situation especially for gay/bi/queer men, even if lesbians, ever resourceful, have been sorting it out in an off-label fashion for a bit longer. So, many sex and gender outlaws are delivered again to this double-edged place: on the one hand, being exiled from the normative methods allows tremendous freedom to create structures or institutions—including families—exactly as we enjoy or prefer them, on our own schedule, including or excluding people based on our own authentic desires rather than on what's expected, typical, or "normal." On the other, whatever we create is assumed to be somehow second-rate, gets no cultural approval and certainly no institutional support. We can build all the families we want, and we can fill them with light and love and fun and freedom, but just like similar delicious and highly customized houses hand-built off the grid, they have no utilities hookups. *No services*, as the real-estate parlance around these kinds of structures puts it.

Eventually, as you might reasonably expect, some people get a little tired of pit toilets and chopping wood and hauling water and driving thirty minutes to town for a latte and a newspaper and a half-cup of Internet access. The relationship-and-family equivalent to that experience is creating the web of documents, wills, trusts, powers-of-attorney, contact lists, and so on that are required for non-mainstream family structures. Exactly as on-the-grid living allows you to call the power company and, assuming you pay your bill, keep the lights on and the hot water flowing, so does institutionally recognized family allow you to get access to parent-teacher conferences and non-taxable inheritance rights just by signing the government-issued piece of paper.

Queers, largely not having had this blood or marriage one-stop situation available to us, have made a virtue of the inevitable and begun enjoying the nicer parts about non-traditional family creation. In some lights we have taken our cues from the ways that religious communities can, over time, begin to feel like families. Many of the people I know who grew up in households headed by straight people with strong ties to religious institutions had Uncle So-and-sos and Auntie Such-and-suchs who weren't bound by blood or marriage but by wine; by the weekly shared observances and the meals that followed. These people understand in a way that's available to many what kind of intimacy grows over time after years of Shabbos meals or Sunday lunches together. Company manners last a while, where everyone keeps their suit-coats and cardigans on and either makes a polite request for glass of water or does without, and the children play quietly some-where out of sight, letting the guest children take the first turn. But slowly, inevitably, the increasing familiarity starts to wear away at everyone's reserve. At some stage, someone says, "Oh, please just feel free to help yourself," and then someone else says, "Why don't you let me bring the chicken?" and someone bullies someone into letting them do the dishes and then one of the kids gets sick or hurt at school and cannot reach a parent. Between bouts of vomiting, when the school nurse asks if there's anyone else at *all* they could call for rescue home to the comfort of pyjamas and room-temperature ginger ale, the kid says, "Maybe my, um, Aunt Lorraine?" "Aunt" Lorraine has a key to the house anyhow, and she's home, and she'll be right over. This seems perfectly okay to all. Our families are who we need when we're beyond helping ourselves. People—gender-normative straight people with all the possible culturally recognized ways of making family available to them—speak un-ironically about their church or mosque or synagogue family, declarations of closeness that can last through generations.

The kids you sneak Shabbos wine with when you're eleven can often become the people at whose weddings you give a toast when you're thirty (if for no other reason than how long they have known you and how many mildly embarrassing stories they can therefore tell on you). The house at which you eat two Sundays a month for your entire childhood, which belongs to your mother's best friend's mother whom you call Granny Linda, becomes a kind of home even if it fails every legal test of whether or not you have the right to access it. And imagine yourself saying, at work, that you need to take a day off for Granny Linda's funeral, when that sad day comes. "Who died?" asks your supervisor. And you fumble, knowing that if this person does not also have a wine family, if they don't have an abiding attachment to what is theirs in heart and spirit but not-theirs by law, they might not understand why you need—legitimately and urgently need—to attend the funeral of someone with whom you have no blood or marriage ties.

Do you gamble and explain, hoping to get approval and increase awareness at the same time? Or do you couch your request in blood-relative terms, posthumously re-assigning Granny Linda as a great-aunt or step-grandmother and thereby securing the right to attend, unchallenged (or at least less-challenged)?

If not blood or marriage, and if not wine—which is extra-legal but heavily validated and valued by the larger culture as we venerate the choice to create religious ties in the first place—then where does that leave queers who are not able to marry and do not choose to join religious communities? Kind of in the cold, culturally speaking. We certainly know that sense of chill as a community, when all the mechanisms of the state exclude us and our people—the marriage equality movement, as its current champions sometimes conveniently forget, started when gay men started dying of AIDS in record numbers and their partners, lovers, best friends, and other kinds of community wound up helplessly locked out of apartments and houses as homophobic parents looted and pillaged, unable to retrieve their own belongings or mementos of their beloved dead. Any legal recourse of the sort that involved producing lease paperwork or receipts for purchased items took months to move through the courts.

(The courts were none too sympathetic anyhow. Recourse through the legal system also involved having heterosexual-style proofs to offer. Joint bank accounts, for example, something not a lot of queers could even get, or co-ownership of big-ticket items like houses or cars with both names of the paperwork were what you needed, and who on earth had that? To say nothing of the reliance in Straightpeoplelandia of certain tropes and proving "real" commitment: living together? Knowing one another's families of origin? Not always.)

Regardless, the need for family remains strong. We want to band together, to get to know each other, to feel connected and close. Especially with bars and clubs so much at the centre of queer people's community life for so long, our spirits yearn for situations where everyone is in their street clothes and day makeup, where there's natural light, where it's quiet enough to make ourselves heard for more than a few sentences worth of come-on, gossip, or shade (or where the main activity isn't stuffing mailings and decrying the patriarchy but enjoying lunch and each other's company).

Glitter family is my long-time favourite term for this: the people who those of us pushed to society's margins (and beyond) make our cohort. Glitter is known to be shiny and unruly, easy to get and hard to be rid of. I love the drag connotations and the femme visibility of it, as well as its unmistakably queer sensibility—look only as far as glitter-bombing for proof that nothing is as thoroughly and satisfyingly queer as glitter. But how is this glitter family made? Where do we find the people that become our glitter family if not through the organized, recognized models demonstrated with the other types?

In some ways, this book is about exactly that. It's about how—how exactly—we make family out of our lovers and our exes and the people we meet at conferences, friends-of-friends that we let stay in our homes or drive to the airport on someone else's say-so and discover that we really enjoy. We find family at our schools and youth groups and bars and squats; sometimes we draw people close after seeing them over and over until one day some connection begins to take root, and sometimes, as Anne Lamott describes in her book *Bird by Bird*: "*Sometimes you run into someone, regardless of age or sex, whom you know absolutely to be an independently operating part of the Whole that goes on all the time inside yourself, and the eye-motes go click... and you recognize them.*" We find our family in failed dates of our own and those of our friends as well, and over the ever-growing Internet, where people we may never have met in person can become family to us.

That's a construction I've always liked, to say that someone is "family to me." I first fell for it when I overheard my friend Robert Lawrence say it on the phone, one of the first times I was in San Francisco visiting and working with him and his equally fabulous partner Carol Queen at the Center for Sex and Culture. I arrived and proceeded to come down with a truly brutal flu—fever and shaking and all. He and Carol were doing quite a bit to keep me from feeling completely bereft, all alone in my slightly seedy motel room with nothing but orange juice and daytime television for company. When I started to feel slightly less wretched, they took me to a Brazilian restaurant and ordered me a feast of meat and vegetables and fresh fruits I couldn't remotely afford, assuring me over my weak protestations that they were going to write it off as CSC business anyhow since I was performing there the next few nights. I ate and drank obediently, mostly listening to them tell me stories about CSC's new home (and attendant new landlord) in a fevered haze.

Then, Robert's phone rang. He made a brief apology and answered it, then he said to the person on the other end that he was at dinner with Carol and Bear, the poor thing, who had come in from out of town to perform and was so sick. I assume that the caller must have either asked if he needed to get off the phone or if he was worried about catching my ick; I couldn't hear and didn't ask. It's his reply that's stuck with me this past decade and gladdened my heart every time I think of it. He said: "No, no, it's all right. Bear's family to me."

Once again, I'd found myself in the family way. Once again, I was so glad of it.

Constellation of Intimates

On our very first date, which I didn't really understand was a date until we were making out in my rental car, Ishai made the most exceptional request of me. He said: "Tell me about your constellation of intimate people."

I had never been asked that before. People had, over the years, frequently asked me "How many people are you involved with, exactly?" based on my relatively public life as a polyamorous person, but they usually turned out to be asking only one of two things. Either they wanted to know if there was any room on my dance card for them, or they wanted to know just how big a slut I really was. Sometimes, both.

Ishai's request, like a lot of the other early indicators about him, was a breath of fresh air. I loved it because it acknowledged and put (thoughtful and lyrical) words to the thing I constantly wrestled with when people asked me questions about my relationships. Namely, that there were people with whom I was very intimately engaged, and people with whom I sometimes had sex, and people who were both, but that sex did not necessarily equal Important Life Person. In fact, over the course of my adult life, my constellation of intimates has been fairly evenly split between people who are or have been lovers and people with whom I have never gone to bed or even come close. I typically had to go the long way around in explaining this, first stating my values around monogamy, friendship and friend networks, and community enmeshment before eventually—if the poor sucker was still listening—talking about my entanglements and intimacies. I never stopped finding it odd that even the most vocal proponents of non-traditional relationship structures typically listed only their lovers as people with whom they were "in a relationship." In retrospect, though, the difficulties of language really do impose themselves on that conversation and a lot of these others: we know to say "this is my husband," and even "this is my husband's girlfriend," but whatever's not culturally valued doesn't get its own words (which is, in some ways, the theme of this whole collection).

So this new, charmingly phrased, and quite sincerely stated request both startled and soothed me. I found myself talking animatedly about the people of whom I am so fond; my boyfriend Bobby and inimitable femme friend Hanne, my partner-in-crime Turner and my good boy Zev, and Kate, my longest love. He didn't ask which of them I was getting naked with, and I don't think I elaborated. I just happily chattered on about how much I liked them and why. Then, when I was finished, I asked the same of him in return. It was a great pleasure (and, I would like to say for the record, was a significant contributing factor to the making-out that shortly followed).

I'm reminded of this conversation every time someone asks me to tell them about my family. This happens to me all the time and for assorted reasons, but most often it's related to my public work. Frequently, the questioner is fishing a little to see if I have any difficult stories about being queer or trans within my family of origin, since that's the most common trope of media coverage of trans people: the terrible part. When I start waxing rhapsodic about the wonderful people in whose orbit I happily make my homes, they interrupt me. "No," they say, looking chagrined. "I, uh ... I meant your real family." When this happens, I prompt them with the phrase "family of origin," and they nod and repeat it gratefully, but honestly, I've already soured on them. I'm tired of the pity narrative, and I lose patience quickly when it's all someone can think to ask about.

Sometimes, though, the question-asking comes from the flip-side. These folks are often the parents of young trans or gender-independent kids, and they are spiky with fear and anxiety that their children won't have the kind of life that those of us who are parents envision for our children; ones with gainful employment, a sweetheart, friends. Some constructions of this future are incredibly rigid and some are tender and flexible, but they all seem to feature the same basic components: belonging, being loved, feeling successful. For these people, my long digression on the wonders of my chosen family—both the closest people and also the folks who are family to me even if we're less often in touch—feel as reassuring to them as they are satisfying to me.

I considered, as I mapped out the essays in this book, devoting a separate chapter to each of a half-dozen people. Individual homages seemed like a pleasant way to spend some time and word count, much as I have in the past opened letters of reference by admitting that I am delighted with a sanctioned opportunity to sing someone's praises without restraint. I want to honour each of these members of my family for what they have been to me and done for me, for all the letters and phone calls and visits and meals, all the occasions of five free minutes of complaint, all the trust and truthfulness and arguing and making up again, all the road trips and late nights lying together in the dark sharing the kind of thoughts we rarely share in the daytime. All of them feel like such treasures to me, both the people and the experiences. I live in a constellation of intimates, and the shape of us is a family. We touch base and check in, with each other and also—I am so gratified to report—they sometimes check in with one another. Correspondences have sprung up and friendships have started to form beyond my influence. Family has begun to take on a transitive property as well.

My desire to devote an individual chapter to each was interrupted by noticing that each of the names appears frequently in this book and the others as well; that the trajectory of our love for one another can be traced through my public work for the past decade. This is true even in places that aren't apparent to the casual reader, and those are—to be perfectly frank—my favourite instances. I treasure my memory of writing the trans-focused smut piece "Payback's a Bitch," eventually published in Tristan Taormino's award-winning anthology *Take Me There*, so that Turner would have something to read at a dirty-story event he had booked us both to read at before realizing that he only had disjointed bits from his performances to rely on, and not even one erotic short story to contribute. I wrote it in the huge clawfoot tub in his old apartment, and then typed it out just before the event. Or seeing a paragraph that I advocated for make the final cut in one of Hanne's books—remembering the turn of phrase I liked so much and being glad to see it again—and also knowing as I work on my edits which paragraph Ishai highlighted as a favourite. Each of the people who are or ever have been my intimates are found in every book and show I've ever written or performed, one way or another, sometimes secretly (turn to page thirteen of my children's book *The Adventures of Tulip, Birthday Wish Fairy* and take a look at the names on the book spines) and sometimes quite legibly, like a big family-wide, worldwide version of the game Bobby and I used to play where we left each other love notes all over the country (about which I wrote a piece in *The Nearest Exit May Be Behind You*).

Suddenly, the idea of a page or even a whole chapter about each of them began to seem uncomfortably reductive. Separate. Like showing you hanks of dyed wool and asking you to imagine how excellent they will be as a finished carpet (an analogy I adore even while I acknowledge that the weaving metaphor has been done to death). Carpets bring a room full of disparate elements together. Carpets are good for warmth and comfort. They add beauty and colour, and they can—if need be—be used to dispose of a dead body. Much like my family. (For the record, I've never asked anyone to help me dispose of a dead body, nor have I been asked, but if the saying is, "A friend will help you move; a true friend will help you move the bodies," I just want to be clear that I think my friends are true indeed). I have driven fifteen hours overnight in the snow when someone's father was in the hospital, I've pretended to be friends with someone's ex in order to better plan their escape from that person, I've learned about Aikido, yoga, the Landmark Forum, graduate programs in seven disciplines, vegan cookery, bipolar disorder, Islam, Buddhism, Spiritualism, non-Hodgkin lymphoma, and educational psychology, and I have purchased—and then FedExed to France—gold lamé size-13.5 high heels. What's also true is that in the moment in which I was doing these things, none seemed particularly onerous. I learned and drove and so on out of love—because when someone you adore wholeheartedly is engaged in something they appreciate, you want to share it with them. Or, at least, I do. And at least as much if not more of this time, care, attention, interest, and learning has been returned to me. It came late to me, this thing of creating relationships that felt as much about being cared for as about caring for someone else, but now that it has finally arrived, I am brimming with that feeling of being held, of being valued, of being loved.

The best thing for me—in all the many gifts of my chosen family, the very best thing—has been feeling that I am seen as the person I am, and loved for it—not measured against old hopes or expectations as I am in my family of origin, but valued for what I've done in the world as the person I am. I can count on my chosen family to understand how big a deal a particular honour or accomplishment is, to talk through complicated problems (especially the kind of problems that really benefit from the advice of an old and close friend who can and will say, at a certain point, "Mister, I love you, but this is just like it was the last four times. We need a different strategy"). They know what I overreact to and what I under-react to, when I'm actually feeling brave and when I'm just putting up a front, when to boss me a little and when to let me go off and do something potentially foolish—all the sorts of intangibles of intimacy that we gain very slowly over time. They can't be rushed; they come with experience and patience—just as my old friend Jonathan, scion of an apple-orcharding family of seven generations, could take one bite of an apple and tell you not just the varietal but how soon it would be ripe, if it was late or early, what kind of weather conditions had contributed to the balance of sweet and tart, and the qualities of the flesh. He would describe the correlation between the rain last year and the taste in my mouth in a way that presaged his choice to later live as a monk for quite some time, and then become a writer after that. It was all there in his eighteen-year-old self, like the apple showing the conditions of his life (and his understanding of even a single, simple apple's nuance, the product of a daily osmosis of information and experience since before he could remember). It's a relief to feel so known, on a level that's both beside and beyond any narrative I might be creating. Especially since I'm so often involved in creating a narrative.

Relief is exactly the right word—my chosen family, and especially my constellation of intimates, is my harbour in the world. Some days I really need one. But it's not just an end-of-the-day sense of relief, the kind where after the travails of a workday you get to finally take your shoes off and put your feet up and have a short measure of something nice and an episode of *The West Wing*. That's a nice thing; it's a pleasure, and over time the daily taste of it contributes to a much longer wellness. But this isn't just that. This kind of relief is also a relief from a lifetime of solitude and doubt. Every phone call and email tells me that all the dire predictions made about my ability to ever make friends or coax anyone into loving me were unfounded. (I already knew they were unkind.) The ways in which the people with whom I have planted and grown great intimacy, whether while naked or dressed or both, make a lie out of the pervasive myth that people like me—fat or queer or trans or unrepentantly nerdy or polyamorous or difficult or some of those things or all of them—that people like me (and maybe like you too) don't get to have families. Not wonderful families, not families full of warmth and heat and light and the clean fresh air of love that lives in the truth. They shame us and scare us; they try to make us normalize ourselves with the threat of loneliness. We resist it so long that then when we can lay down our arms, sometimes we just need to cuddle up and cry for a while (or at intervals, forever), and having a way to do that is as much a pleasure as the first moment a painful injury finally doesn't hurt anymore—the relief radiates like the sun.

There's another kind of relief worth mentioning here: the relief of having such an important thing named and recognized so well. When Ishai asked me about my constellation of intimates, I also felt the relief of not having to start at zero and explain everything I value and cherish in the world of relationships. It was a shibboleth; I knew immediately that despite the fact he'd offered me something called a vegan Reuben sandwich, we were nevertheless together in a profound way on some of the most important issues in my universe. I walked through the door he held open for me that afternoon, to that wobbly little café table, and into a whole new wonderful life.

Sperm Agreement/Holding the Line against Grandparents

For a while, there was a by-product for us in creating Stanley and making this wonderful little family which we didn't expect or plan for: we became very interested in drawing a bright and clear boundary between The Family and The Rifkins. On the one hand, we adore Spuncle Jacob, and we really did want him to be the other genetic contributor to our small person. But on the other hand, we'd heard endless horror stories of donors and their family members creating nightmare scenarios of custody agreements and legal wrangling, and Ishai and I were terrified of ending up in a similar situation. We'd considered true anonymous donation, but ultimately had to acknowledge our own (very personal) discomfort with the idea of choosing a stranger's gametes to make a family with. Using a donor we knew, or even a cocktail made from a couple of donors we had chosen, turned out to give us what we wanted in a maker-of-sperm: some level of knowability, and some sense of the human our eventual child might someday resemble in looks or manner or, in the best-case scenario, spirit. So once we'd chosen Jacob, the person whose gonads we intended to borrow to complete our scheme, we began to understand that with the sperm came the man, and with the man came his family.

As quickly became apparent, we needed to talk about a few things. First, we talked a lot about obligations and prohibitions,

since we're all nerdy Jews, and one of the questions that interests the Jewish legal system most is that of obligations and prohibitions: What I am required to do? What am I forbidden from
doing? That's what makes up any sort of contract in any legal
system, as well as most of the less-formal compacts and agreements we hammer out specifically or suss out tacitly in all kinds
of relationships. Knowing the hard yeses and the hard noes is also
a good way to see the edges of a new agreement of any sort, right?
It defines the room in which we have to work, or live, or even love.

With this in mind, and with many years of study and preced-
ent to guide us, we started talking about the questions related to
then-unnamed, still-theoretical Stanley. I wish I could go back in
time and watch the video of us doing this. I imagine it would have
been fairly funny to any more knowledgable being that might have
been watching. Some of the things we worried about were pretty
ridiculous, and some things we didn't concern ourselves with we
probably should have. Nevertheless, it was a good undertaking—
worthwhile in that it got us to a place where we could talk deeply
about what was beneath the various rules we were setting. Ishai
and I feared non-consensual incursions from Jacob's family into
our lives; or that he or his parents might sue for custody, that they
might try to usurp our authority or decision-making as parents.

(It's worth mentioning that we had not met his family at the
time of this conversation, which in retrospect would have helped
a lot—if for no other reason than that we would have been better
able to see we were projecting our fears onto the blank screen
in our minds marked *The Rifkins* [note to the reader: not recom-
mended]. This had nothing to do with the actual Rifkins, who
in real life are two of the kindest, most tender-hearted humans
you might ever have the good fortune to meet, and it was quickly

apparent to us how their son Jacob turned out to be so great.)

I had a recurring nightmare that involved Jacob meeting an untimely death and his parents attempting to reclaim his bloodline by coming to visit and then kidnapping our child back to Kansas (and therefore did a lot of deeply disheartening research on custody laws in Kansas). I'm not actually sure where we got these fears from—Lifetime Made-For-TV movies with Ripped From The Headlines™ plots? But somehow we had this idea that we needed to guard our parenting territory fiercely, lest someone swoop down and try to forbid us from vaccinating our eventual small child or force us to raise him in the US. So even though we knew that a document of intention is not a legally binding document, especially before the birth if a child, we drew one up anyhow.

We carefully discussed and mapped out various scenarios: Would Jacob be able to express his opinions about certain things, if he didn't try to enforce them? Would we rather he kept them entirely to himself? How about money—we'd agreed that he had no obligation, but what if he wanted to contribute to a college fund? Would this buy him the rights to participate in university-related decisions for this child when the time eventually came? How often would he want to see the kid? How would he refer to our child, and what might our child call him? It required us to project ourselves together into a long future, and to try to be both realistic and also kind to our future selves. We recognized and wrote in, for example, our expectation that, as our child got older, kid and Spuncle would be able to do some planning and sorting out of their own visits, independent of us, and that this was to be encouraged. I would say we were generous and optimistic; that we tried to create a balance between making room for some possibilities while discouraging others. The number one thing Ishai and I were trying to discourage was any chance that Jacob—whose contribu-tion was to be critical but brief—would begin to imagine himself as one of the parents of this child. He was going to have two dads already. Spuncle Jacob was what we could offer him.

But. What *about* his parents, while we were on the topic? We'd heard his story of telling them, once Ishai was five months pregnant, that he had loaned us a cup of sperm for our grand, child-raising adventure and that they had been supportive and welcoming of this news. At the time, they had no grandchildren, and I think they considered Jacob's choice to be in keeping with their values (loving parents, Jewish home, sufficient resources) enough to support it wholeheartedly. I haven't asked them about this directly, in order to preserve some bit of their interior lives from us, if not from my gentle readers. What if they had grave misgivings at first? What if they still harbour some doubts or fears about this arrangement? That would certainly be legitimate, especially considering that they have no other grandchildren yet. Are they perhaps holding onto Stanley's existence as a comfort against any concern they might feel that they'll never been given more ... legit grandchildren?

I don't want to ask these questions directly. They've always been very nice to us and they clearly adore Stanley, so I'm not in a big hurry to start interrogating (also, I strongly suspect that none of these fears are true and I'd just wind up offending them for even thinking it). But all these prospects were in the mix when we sat down in the fall of 2008 to start imagining how, whether, and when we could potentially make ourselves a Stanley.

Jacob's own involvement was relatively delineated for us in most places, but the questions surrounding a potential third set of grandparents were harder to parse out. Once Ishai and Jacob coaxed me past my natural tendency to run to the worst-case scenario, we settled into planning and preparing. The question of what Stanley might call his parents came up, as did things like: What would happen when or if Jacob had children of his own? Would we call them Stanley's half-siblings? Cousins? Would Jacob's brother's possible eventual children be cousins as well? How would we make sense of this? Did Jacob think his parents would want to meet Stanley? Develop a relationship with him? How would our own parents (Ishai's and mine) feel about a third set of grandparents in the mix? We ate and drank and discussed it, somehow understanding that the time to address this situation was now, while everyone had been getting plenty of sleep.

(In some ways, this is an exceptionally Jewish choice—in just the same way that a traditional Jewish marriage contract specifies the terms of divorce if they're ever needed. We plan in love and hope for the possibility of disaster; we know it makes the settlements more equitable, and also no one wants to wrangle around in these choices when they can't even agree on small things anymore. People sometimes report that they find this particular Jewish practice unromantic, but to me it makes perfect sense.)

Eventually, six months later—through a combination of love, luck, and a fortuitously timed gallbladder incident—we were embarked for good on our adventure in Advanced Placement Family Dynamics. Ishai and I got married, Jacob explained to his parents what we had done, the baby was born and named, and in short order colonized all of our hearts with pure love. We were very lucky in this way, it must be said. There are any number of stories in which family choices are not greeted warmly by families of origin. My parents and Ishai's too were over the moon with excitement—at one point I described my mother as beside herself and then beside *that* self in her anticipation—which made an enormous difference in how the period leading up to Stanley's arrival (and immediately afterward too) went. My brother Jeffrey, just as effusive a person as I am in the face of good news, told everyone he was going to be an uncle and never expressed the slightest concern about all the other people who were going to be sharing his title (or some variant of it) with him.

But also, after all the talking and thinking and pre-negotiation, we all knew that there was every possibility people could start changing their minds or attempting to revise previous agreements. What if Jacob decided he wanted to be a Father, capital-F style, right then? What if someone's parents went Cuckoo for Cocoa Puffs and tried to initiate a custody proceeding on the grounds that a pair of queer polyamorous trans men were *not* fit to raise a child? What if some other horror we hadn't yet considered came to pass?

They were all good and valid questions, but none of them happened. Instead, we found ourselves in the thrall of Stanley, all being able to relax our vigilance and concerns. I stopped worrying about whether it would be too "dad-like" for Jacob to do some-thing-or-other, and I relaxed further when I saw that both my parents and Ishai's had figured out a way to treat Jacob that was warm and familial but not ... well, weird. We spoke to the Rifkins on the phone and sent them a stream of photos of Stanley's first days, his *bris*, and I found myself able to include lots of pictures of Jacob holding him, looking delighted—a photo I had previously been against for some reason I could no longer remember. Everyone posed with the baby, our giant and beautiful son with his dark open eyes and full head of hair, who held

44

his own head up immediately and regarded everyone with an expression of great interest as though he were a teensy anthropologist from another universe.

When the Rifkins asked if they could share the photos with their friends and relatives we said *of course*, realizing only sometime much later that people across the states of Missouri and Kansas were all getting a brief but tender lesson on transmasculine reproduction and family creation. Courtesy of us. When they asked if they could send toys we said *of course,* and when they asked if we might like to spend a little time with them at an event for Jacob's ordination as a rabbi that spring we said *of course* again—because who on earth wouldn't want to let every possible person adore this little miracle we'd made? They were thoughtful and a little hesitant, never assuming anything or arrogating to themselves the traditional rights of grandparents. Their choice to hang back a bit left all kinds of room for us to be generous, and it no longer seemed so important to draw this bright line between them and the other grandparents. Things had shifted after the birth of the baby, as we'd expected, but no one had anticipated the direction in which they were going to shift.

Suddenly we were left holding this question that had seemed urgent just a few days ago—what role would the Rifkins play in Stanley's life? It had deflated as surely as had all our other fears and upsets from the pre-baby time. Now, we had a whole *new* set of things to worry about, but none of them was whether anyone would possibly want or love or attach themselves to this kid too much. We both wanted all the help we could get and found it perfectly understandable that people were entranced by him. There was no problem anymore. Once we were ready to stop guarding the battlements, we noticed that the war had never materialized.

So we went downstairs and let down the drawbridge and sent the dragons all home.

In retrospect, it seems sort of hilarious that I—the intimacy junkie, the one who would make family out of anyone if I had that kind of time, who is endlessly trumpeting on about chosen families—found it in myself to try to steel myself against the (completely theoretical) incursions into my family life of two perfectly lovely fifty-something Jewish educators from Kansas. I can see it through life's rearview mirror as a function of my fear—both about being a parent and also about protecting both the integrity and the legitimacy of my family. I knew that queer and trans parents, as well as pagan parents and atheist parents and sexual outlaw parents and all sorts of non-normative folks, have lost the right to parent their children because of a narrow-minded legal decision. I was ready to take up arms to keep that from coming to pass, which, to no one's surprise but my own, it didn't (or hasn't yet). We know people for whom it has, though, or nearly. Two years ago, a lesbian colleague of Ishai's on vacation with her wife and daughters got brutalized by the Child Protective Services system when a homophobic stranger called CPS and made up wild stories about what she suspected they were doing, based on nothing more than the fact that they were lesbian mums. More recently, some friends from our gay dads group reported that they'd been questioned in their hotel room at a resort in the Caribbean, where they were vacationing with their three sons, about where the boys had come from and what they were doing with them. It's enough to make anyone paranoid, even people who have further to go than me.

Now in my general state of relaxation about the issue (or as much relaxation as I'm prone to, let's be honest), I shake my head

46

at myself. I know what I was so worried about, but it seems terribly unlikely. Stanley is growing up in the centre of a huge group of family, biological and logical, aunties and uncles and a spuncle and some sparkles, and all manner and sort of other people. None of them detracts anything from the others, they all add; they all give him new gifts of love and attention and small pointy things for his parents to step on in the middle of the night. Would there not seem to be room at the table for one Grandspuncle and one Grandsparkle to join the fun and adore their Sparkling?

Of course there is. I don't regret the time we spent on our agreements and intentions, I really don't. I learned a lot from it, and we got to some very good and useful places as we talked. It's nice to have my fears calmed, though. Even if my nerves are a little jangled just now from the ongoing noise of a forty-nine-key pressure-sensitive electronic keyboard—a gift from Grandspuncle and Grandsparkle. Oh, well. Noisy toys were never covered in the agreement, anyhow.

Comforter

In the week after Stanley is born (which is also the week leading up to his *brit milah*, when we will have him circumcised and give him his Hebrew name), my mother comments to me how funny it is that so many people are so excited about his arrival, about Ishai and me as parents. Cards and parcels and phone calls have been streaming in all week; all manner of floral arrangements crowd the tops of bookshelves, and the ceiling has developed quite the crop of balloons. At first, I absorb and dismiss her comment as the musing of someone with no online life—someone who has never either friended or unfriended, with no first-hand experience of the kinds of intimacies that can develop over the interwebs. Sure she's surprised; she knows only the people she actually knows, in person, in real life. It's no bad thing, just a different paradigm. She hasn't accounted for the extra traffic of 2,500 fans, acquaintances, and "friends."

At the end of that first bewildered and sleep-deprived week, with our tiny living room crammed with guests and food, we give Stanley the Hebrew name Menachem. We have always known he would be named Stanley. Ishai and I both had grandfathers named Stanley with whom we were close and who died within a few months of each other; our firstborn child's name was never really in question (even if he'd been a girl, he would have been Stanley, a first name she would have shared with Stanley Ann Dunham, the mother of Barack Obama). But in the choice of Hebrew names, the name by which our Jewish child will be called at many of the major events of his life, we take some liberties. It's quite usual to give a child the Hebrew equivalent of hir English name as a Hebrew name, but it's not required and honestly, whenever there's a chance to remix the traditions with some new ideas, we are the people to choose that option. And so, we take the chance to give our son a name that speaks of the qualities we see in him. Menachem means comforter, and we both love that. We love it for its gravitas in the mouth, and for the hope it seems to carry that he could be of comfort to others. We like the idea that our boy-child, our little incipient white man, could over his lifetime internalize the idea that a man could and should create comfort and solace in his world. Then too, there is the new and peaceful look on Ishai's face. After years of yearning to be a parent, of trying and being thwarted on so many levels, here is the answer to hundreds of prayers: little Menachem, a comfort. Our comforter.

It's perfect, and we're full up with the perfection of him and how much we feel as though he has brought so many wonders with him. The cards and letters and calls keep coming; offers to visit are really command performances with the new small person. Ishai and I remain delightedly bathed in the love of our community, if perhaps also delirious from the lack of sleep. Are calls and cards and Facebook comments still rolling in? Didn't some of those arrive yesterday, or last week? I'm not entirely certain. I rock our son and walk our dog and bake fresh bread, and when the boyo sleeps, I work on the huge anthology I'm editing, and when my mother comments again that so many people are so excited about Stanley, I don't remember what I say in reply. I am really very, very tired.

Over the months that follow, though, I start to wonder. Certainly

I've had plenty of exposure to those folks of my community whose feelings about children and child-raising can be summed up under the general heading of "Thank Maude I don't have to worry about that anymore." I knew a lot of people who resented the whole business; some who fumed over the attention that was paid to the spawn of their heterosexual siblings, and some who simply didn't care to spend their time with anyone too young to appreciate a well-made cocktail. And as a queer who has been out in queer social circles my entire adult life, I expected that some of those friends would just disappear when our son was born, or drop us from their party-invite lists, or simply make excuses never to have to come over, ever again, ever. (I just figured, well, you can't have everything.) Anyway, my attention was pretty well commanded by this brand-new person we made (and also the anthology I was still editing, using every ounce of non-baby-related concentration I could summon). But as the weeks passed, as I began to get longer chunks of sleep, and as the sense of vagueness about the days started to lift, people started saying things I never expected.

Our friend Kate immediately announced that she would be Stanley's Fairy Godsmother, and that she intended to take her role very seriously. Our other friend Kate said, "You know, I'm not really that excited about children. But I'm very excited about you and Ishai having a child. Do I get to be Auntie Kate?" We certainly opened up the field and encouraged friends and relatives to declare their relationship to Stanley on their own terms, and we were overwhelmed and delighted with the results. People chose their own titles, with the range of whimsy and thoughtfulness I have come to expect from my friends and family—Big Pup, Sparkle, Fairy Godsmother, and so on—but with an urgency that was a little startling, all of them demanding our promises that we would bring Stanley to see them frequently, supply regular photographic evidence of his excursions large and small, show their photos to him so he doesn't forget what they look like, arrange Skype dates so that they can read him stories at night from Alaska, Barcelona, San Francisco, New York, Baltimore, and so on. My good boy Zev, who works all over Europe and Africa, started up a campaign to make certain that Stanley had the most extensive collection of international T-shirts the world had ever known while he proudly displayed Stanley's photo everywhere he went and bragged about his eldest nephew. The meanest BDSM top I know or have ever known, a woman whose primary DIY handicraft heretofore had been bending spinal-tap needles into tight spirals for use in anchoring volunteer body parts to their neighbours like a binding comb, knit Stanley a bib with a dinosaur pattern. And mailed it Global Express, yet—lest the little dude be deprived of his Stegosaurus intarsia accessory for three more days.

It begins to appear that my mother was not as mistaken as I originally thought.

It was settled the day that my boyfriend Bobby—the one who is nearly afraid of small children, who said in the first years of our relationship before I met and married Ishai that he preferred children to be raised in isolation until they were five at the very least—said to me when we're arranging a visit: "Are you bringing our little Stanley?"

I had to sit down when I heard this. "Our little Stanley?" I repeated, full of wonderment, "Are you kidding me?"

He's not. No one is. As I ask people what's brought about the changes in their attitudes, the answer I get most often is that in fact there's no change. It's just this little guy ... somehow he's not the same category as Children. Slightly defensive answers drift off into fond and tender meditations about how people regard Ishai and I as a pair of parents: how tender-hearted, how very engaged with issues of equity and justice and liberation, how community-minded we both are. Dreamily, more than one person says how much they wished they could have been raised by parents like us, queer parents, trans parents; how much they wish their family tree had been like Stanley's will be—branches dripping with courtesy uncles and aunts (and sparkles and pups and so on), full of people who are ready to like him as he is. Not to mention blood family—especially my brother Jeffrey and Ishai's sister Bronwen—who couldn't be more pleased to share their Stanley-adoring duties with a multi-national, multi-gendered cast of big-hearted characters such as they do, who have been as generous about sharing the love as they are thoughtful about making friends with the other people Stanley is regularly thrilled to see or hear from. Who want to meet him and raise him up into who he will be. One friend mentions how many faith communities are represented in our inner circle and someone else says that no matter what sort of hobby or diversion Stanley chooses, some one of his beloved people probably knows how already and will be glad to teach him.

Of course, this is an idealized view of us as parents; we are just as likely as any other parents to get frustrated or lose patience with preschool shenanigans. But they are also our ideal—that is, what we're hoping for. After thinking a lot, and carefully, about what kind of parents we want to be and what kind of values we want to model, Ishai and I have focused our parenting energies (those left over after keeping him from falling off all the things he can climb up and trying to get enough food into him) on creating a world for Stanley which is full of love, and full of options. All kinds of models. All kinds of people to adore him.

We chose this method because we thought it would suit us and him, our cheerful little chatterbox boy, our vertical adventurer. What we didn't understand was how it would affect other people. Our choices and our attempts at thoughtful parenting, which are transparent as Ishai and I write and talk about them publicly and privately, turn out also to soothe some injured place in many of the people with whom we are closest. Some of them are the self-determined results of terrible parenting—some criminally terrible, some just utterly self-absorbed—some the children of people whose ability to parent crumpled in the face of a queer or trans kid. They were damaged by their childhoods, in many cases. They didn't feel loved, or they still don't. Childhood, or young adulthood, was a misery to be endured. No wonder they don't want children—if they had children, they would have to be parents, and parents are not the kind of people they want to be.

For some, yes, it's that parents wake up at seven a.m. most days of the week and can't go to the theatre or sex parties unless they can secure a babysitter. But for others, I finally understand, it's that their only experience of parents is their own, and they simply cannot imagine embodying something that has damaged them so. I get it now.

Then along comes Stanley, our sunny, sweet baby boy who is also named Menachem, comforter, and it's totally clear to me in a flash that we gave him exactly the right name. That in addition to priming him with the idea that he can be a comfort, volitionally, as a man, he is in fact a comfort already. That's why the outpouring of community support has been so huge; that's why people all but fight over the opportunity to be with him while Ishai and

I have a grown-up evening—he embodies the idea that not all childhoods have to be miserable. If he turns out queer or trans or whatever new identity marker we'll have in twenty years, he won't be turned out of the house, except to get off to university or trade school or travel. He'll never be shunted off to foster care, or locked in a cupboard, or belittled as too femme-y or too butch. He was planned for and adored from the first moment, he has been handed around to all comers to be adored since he was an hour old. Through this he learns the world: big bearded tattooed men are wonderful snugglers and do not mind when you yank on their beards or giant aught-gauge earrings, grandmother-aged women rather do mind when you pull on their earrings but often have necklaces to play with; dreadlocks are not for chewing; silver cuff bracelets make great cymbals; hands out of the hijab, please, little one. All of this is his daily experience of love. He makes family look like something we can all do, no matter how hard it was the first time. Comfort, indeed.

Karma

I admit it: as a newly out queerlet of sixteen or so, full of the first stirrings of queer pride, living in a suburban, white enclave, I looked for opportunities to come out. No one, no matter how innocuous their hetero-assumptive comment, was safe from me and my relentless outness. I printed a list of Gays Throughout History and carried it in my schoolbag, lest I miss an opportunity to discuss a gay or lesbian historical figure. I wore my pink triangle pin everywhere—pink triangles, for those of you under thirty, is what we had before the rainbow as the international symbol of Queers Here—and you can bet I explained to anyone who asked about it (or frankly, even glanced at it) what it was for, complete with full-bore Holocaust imagery and my fresh new Queer Nation vocab. Woe betide those like the nice lady at the Mailboxes Etc. counter, to whom I presented the Valentine's package for my first girlfriend. Seeing it festooned with sparkle hearts and love haiku, she surmised aloud that my boyfriend would be so excited by my gift. She would have been lucky if I'd just grabbed up my box o' love and exited in a homo huff. Instead, I stood there and lectured her for quite some time about heterosexism and homophobia.

I hope it wasn't for more than a few minutes, but as I said, I was sixteen, and even more of an insufferable know-it-all than I am now. When I finally ground to a breathless halt, totally over-revved with the exhilaration of having stood up for myself and advocated on behalf of My People, she said, gently:

I'm a lesbian myself. Are we sending this Priority Mail?

Um. Yes. Priority Mail will be fine, thank you.

I came out of the closet in a self-righteous rush, and kept right on coming out for several years. It was a hobby, of sorts, and nearly always entertaining, even when—or maybe especially when—it resulted in a theological argument or some sort of condemnation. Few things are as satisfying, when you're a young activist who is often called to testify about the impact of homophobia, as the actual tales of homophobes who shout at you in the condiment aisle that you're going to hell. If I might have skipped recounting what I shouted at them first, perhaps you will forgive me.

Karma, on the other hand, does not seem to have forgiven me. I know this because now, twenty years later (G-d help me) I have this very charming small son who rides over my shoulder when we go out on errands, and smiles his great big wonderful smile at all manner of my co-erranders. And then they want to talk to me about him, which is lovely, because he is a favourite topic of conversation. Unfortunately, they also want to talk about his mother, the person who is also evidently my wife, and this is awkward. Because neither such person exists. And so now—when I don't really have the time my sixteen-year-old self had for extended comings-out, when I am juggling my packages and my wriggly, twenty-pound five-month-old, when I have quickly cooling drool running down the back of my neck—now I have to take the time to come out. Multiple times per day. That sound you hear? That's Karma, laughing her fucking ass off.

I got my practice out on the soccer field of my local park, walking the dog with Stanley—then ten days old—asleep on my chest in his groovy baby wrap, zipped into my hoodie with me for extra warmth and comfort in the February early-morning chill. When

I reappeared among the eight a.m. dog-walk crew, now looking very tired and strangely ... lumpy, from a distance, they were all curious and then delighted. Women, groups of women, plucked at my clothes and reached out to unzip my hoodie. All so they could catch a glimpse of baby Stanley, but I didn't mind.

Because I'd been coming to the dog park for a year and change by that point, some of the other dog-walkers knew I was of the homo variety. Their questions were mostly along the theme of "Where did you get that baby?" (The stork brought him, said with a shrug and a grin, was my favourite answer.) But by and large, my fellow dog walkers wanted to know how my wife was doing, and whether she knew I had the baby out In This Weather. Often, one of the dog walkers I knew a little better—Watson's person, perhaps, or Charlie and Coko's person—would step in and say, "Oh, he has a husband," which delivered me back into "Where did you get that baby?" territory again. Second verse, same as the first.

It's in places of public commerce and entertainment that I find myself most likely to be assumed heterosexual until proven other-wise, both at sixteen and now. In the supermarket, with Stanley—then three months old—riding along in his infant carrier, one clerk apparently just could not contain herself. For most of my groceries we didn't talk, but by the time she picked up a can of chickpeas she seemed unable to resist any longer, and burst out with: "When you find a job, will your wife stay home with the baby?"

(There's an idiomatic French phrase, *l'esprit d'escalier*, which refers to what you realize, far too late for it to do you any good, what you *ought* to have said in retort to someone at some previ-ous time. This—this and being peed on—are the two things about having a baby that I could frankly do without.)

Never mind what I said in reply. It wasn't really very funny, nor did I take her to task. In my defense, I was sleeping very little at that stage. But, oh my stars and garters, do people ever love to ask those sorts of questions. It's as though secretly, everyone is living in an episode of *The Brady Bunch* and everyone knows it but me.

On the flipside, straight strangers more frequently want to have a chat. Gone are the days when I, as a burly dude in jeans and tank boots, made women look behind them and put a surreptitious hand on their purses, and even longer gone are my late, great bulldagger days, when as a burly dyke (in jeans and tank boots) people snickered, stared, and pretended they weren't pointing. These days, when I am out in the company of my small son I am a dad, and therefore a whole different category of person. The same straight women who quailed at the sight of me for the better part of two decades, for whatever their reasons, now march right over to me—well, really they march right over to Stanley, he's the main attraction, I am merely the baby *wallah*, but still—and show no fear as they make smiley faces and cooing noises at my small son.

Not only that, but coming out as gay no longer seems to deter them. Sign of the times, maybe, or the automatic de-sexualizing that we culturally attach to parents, who we assume are too sleepy to get any really sinful shenanigans going anyhow. The addition of my cheerful, drooling son slung over my shoulder in his customary ride-along spot moves me from leering outlier of the homosexual underworld to an emissary from the well-known, well-travelled Land of Dad. If I happen to be from one of the pinker neighbourhoods, no matter. There I am, fuzzy animal hanging out of my back pocket and spit-up down my sleeve: obviously acceptable.

Nonetheless, I come out and come out and come out again, not ready to just nod along with heterosexual identifiers and discuss the imaginary wishes or wellness of my imaginary wife. I have to confess, however, that though I always come out as queer, I do not always really explain where, exactly, *this* baby has come from. "The stork brought him" is in some measure my way of letting people know that their personal questions about my son's provenance are not welcome, but it's also how I avoid—without lying—the long-form explanation. Yes, I'm a homo. Married to another homo. No, the baby isn't adopted. No, nor a foster child either. How is this possible? Well. Do you have a minute?

It takes more than a minute. There's no short, "Well, when two transsexuals love each other veeeery, very much, they give each other a *special* hug ..." kind of an answer. I started out, two years, two books, and one little boy ago, saying to people, "Oh, my husband's a transsexual, and he still has his uterus, so we're going homemade." That was before I was carrying an infant around, so I had time to sort through the aftermath of the revelation with them, decoupling sex from gender (and both of them from fucking) and then justifying our decision. These days, I have ninety minutes to get all the errands done before naptime. I come out queer, charmingly evade all inquiries about where we got Stanley ("At Babies R Us. They were having a sale"), agree that yes, he is unusually cute, and start edging toward the organic bananas or the peanut-butter dog biscuits with an apologetic smile. They understand. They remember the tyranny of naptime. We're all in this together.

And so I go, gaily, with my son, and that brings enough questions as it is. At Starbucks, when he was four months old, I strolled in with him riding in his soft carrier, again snug on my chest and smiling away at everyone around him like a half-pint-sized Miss

America. We got me an iced coffee and him several lavish compliments on his general-duty magnificence from the baristas, who are among the many, many members of his worldwide fan club. On the way out, a woman of roughly my age stopped us to tickle the bottoms of his feet while saying to me, "Ooh, you look so *cute* together! I could never get my husband to take either of our kids out in that thing. He looks so comfortable in it! How did your wife get you to use it?"

"Well," I replied, "I have a husband. So I imagine that changes the game a little."

Sagely, she nodded, then smiled and said—in a tone which clearly suggested that she wanted to say something that would let me know she understood—"Ohhh. So you're the woman-gay."

Across the screen in my brain flashed the first three points of my argument: I have grown since I was sixteen, but haven't changed that much. I wanted to tell her, Miss Clueless Suburbia 2010, that that wasn't at all how it worked, and that queers were not in any way required to abide by some sort of imitation-heterosexual gender-role division system, and that furthermore, as a feminist myself, I was disturbed by her intimation that caring for a child was women's work, and perhaps *that* was why her husband didn't want to wear their children in carriers out in public, if she felt that way about it, and while we were at it, just a general note, honey, that Starbucks was full of mothers out with their children and even though society doesn't value the work of child-raising when it's done by mothers, because we just think that's their *job*, all those moms out with their kids were also very cute and very fabulous and where was the love for them, hey?

This is the good thing about being a professional educator, right? The talking points are always ready to go. I opened my mouth to begin making her really regret her choice of words and worldviews.

And then Stanley spit up in my ear.

"It doesn't really work that way," I said, simply, accepting the napkin she handed me and shifting the kiddo to my other side. I crammed it as deep into my ear as I could, for maximum spit-up absorbency and to drown out the appalled sixteen-year-old me I could hear faintly, howling in outrage, from twenty years ago. "We worked hard to make sure we both get lots of time with him. My husband took—"

She interrupted me, patting my tanned forearm, newly muscular from carrying a squirmy, chunky infant around all the time. "Well, whatever," she said, sort of dismissively. I could have pressed on, but it turns out that at a certain point, getting a warm response about being a gay dad out with your son can be enough for one day. Sometimes when this happens I feel a pang of regret for not taking more time to educate, to come out some more as a trans-parent, to use my opportunity for more education. I wish I had more time and energy to do it. I certainly have plenty of chances, many of which are not scuppered by spit-up in my ear. I resolved in that moment to do better next time—to explain more, to make more space for all kinds of families in the world, for all kinds of parents and all the kids they love and all the ways they got them.

She gave Stanley one more wide grin and, getting an equally exuberant one in return, said, "He's *incredibly* cute. And that smile! He looks just like you, really."

Next, next time, I meant. When I don't have spit-up in my ear. This time, I just shook my head, and laughed, and told a different truth: I said, "People tell me that all the time."

What They See

This is exactly what happens. An editor writes to ask, "Would you like to write for my publication? About being a dad? Something interesting, please," and being interesting sounds like a challenge you're up for, especially after suffering none-too-gracefully through several terrible books designed for expectant fathers, one of which used the euphemism "sweater puppies." So you write back and zealously if stupidly propose a series of pieces aimed at expectant fathers, each touching on an aspect of being a dad that no one tells you shit about before the kid arrives (these things are legion). Maybe half a dozen of them, you say to this editor, in the full flower of optimism. This seems like a great idea to her, and to you, too. You promptly sit down and write the first six hundred words of this proposed essay, trying to simultaneously strike a calming tone and tell the unvarnished truth about the reality of being a parent. While bogged down in the terminological problem of trying also to inclusively address lesbian non-gestational co-parents while maintaining a breezy, manly tone, your toddler wakes up from his nap and demands something.

(Toddlers live in a perpetual state of demanding something. This is partly because they just learned how to say what they want and partly because their language skills pretty much begin and end in the declarative. The experience of living with a teensy emperor passes eventually. I hear.)

Weeks pass. If this were the movies, tumbleweeds would roll

across the abandoned page (it's not unlike writing a book, as it happens). It's perfectly serviceable but no longer feels fresh or urgent and so it gets put aside in favour of other deadlier deadlines, or getting the laundry somewhat under control or trying to determine if your son can wait until the weekend for new boots or if you really need to go after work tonight and get them.

This is a thing that happens, by the way, one of the many things no one tells you—they just shoot up overnight. One day all your kid's pants are a fine size, reaching all the way to his shoes, and then next day they're all capris. You find yourself sort of squinting at them one morning, trying to determine how long they've been like that, really? No time at all. Don't worry; they do this.

They do a lot of things. This morning my son, who is a shade over two, woke up, announced "It's not dark. It's day," and proceeded in short order to smack me in the nose with a book he wanted read to him, push several towels off the upstairs gallery railing down onto the dog sleeping on the sofa below (thereby waking her up and freaking her out), drop and break a wooden dolphin and then cut himself on the resulting sharp edge, make the alarm clock go off in the guest room, and flush the toilet fourteen times. This is at 7:20 a.m. on a Sunday, you understand.

(Another thing they don't really mention about having a kid—they have no respect for the lazy weekend morning for quite some time.)

In any event, when Sunday mornings start like this at our house, we activate what we refer to as the Emergency Pastry Protocol, which is that whichever parent is marginally more functional changes the kid into a dry diaper, puts socks and shoes and a jacket on him, tosses him in the car still otherwise in his PJs, and heads halfway across the city to our very favourite bakery for morning things, the place of croissants that are still warm when they open at eight a.m. and are taken from an old wooden box and put into a fresh paper bag. The kid loves this place. They love him back, too, and always greet him by name, in his dinosaur pyjamas and his winter coat, like a very honoured guest.

So there we are, having come inside out of the rain at ten minutes after eight this very morning, with the small person set on Rambunctious and the big person (me) struggling to keep up. Monsieur Rambunctious issues further demands:

"I want to eat! I want to sit in a chair! I want to sit in a chair and eat my kah-sunt!"

I settle him in a chair, then I re-settle him elsewhere when he—channelling his inner Diva—insists that he requires a different chair. I put him in it, give him a piece of croissant to start with, and go to stand in line to pay. He remains seated for some unit of time too small to measure with common chronological instruments and then gets up and starts to wander around. The bakery is tiny, and packed, and little man has his mouth crammed full of croissant as he cheerfully and completely ignores my quiet instructions to please sit back down, or come here, or holy crapping tadpoles please just please stop touching everything in the whole wide world one by one.

He's clearly in his own world, his long curls all but covering one half of his face, munching contemplatively with a tin of sardines in his hand. I'm getting progressively more cross, because he's not responding to my instructions at all, and that is one of my least favourite toddler behaviours. Out of the corner of my eye I see movement, a gesture that my parental sixth sense tells me is related to my son, so I turn to look.

There's a guy over by the fix-your-coffee-how-you-like-it

station. He has indicated the little dude to his partner, and is smiling at her. She reaches out and takes his hand, and smiles back at him and in this moment I realize that she is at least eight months pregnant, and that they are both looking at my kid with faces of delight and anticipation as he gets crumbs all over the floor and all down the front of his pyjamas and wanders over at his own glacial pace to stand beside me and lean his sleep-tousled head on my thigh. Still eating his croissant, still clutching a can of sardines.

Oh. Right. They don't see what I see at all. They don't see how he won't sit still and isn't listening and is covered in a mush of crumbs and smears of butter and raindrops. They see how he's eating well and watching everything and is confidently taking jars of jam off the lowest shelves, inspecting them, and placing them back on the shelf with the less-buttery hand. When he reaches up to me with one of the jars and says, "Papa! This is a boo-berry jam, Papa! Is it yummy?" the man gives the woman a look of such love and longing it kind of spears me through the heart a little bit. I remember that moment of perfect expectation, before the mess and sleeplessness set in.

There. That's the first thing no one tells you about being a dad (or the lesbian equivalent): you're so fucking lucky, you shouldn't be able to stand yourself most of the time. That's your kid. Your amazing kid who adores you, even when he's kicking you in the ear or trying to stick his buttery fingers in your eye (and certainly smearing them all over your glasses), and the fact that he won't sit down and refuses to listen is totally immaterial. They never sit down, and they hardly listen. They're still magic. Try very hard to remember.

(interstitial)

Hi.

Some of you are reading along and going, "Huh, this is interesting," and some think, "Yes, this feels familiar," and still others of you are probably thinking, "How many more chapters of this do I have to read before Tuesday?" and a last subset are thinking, "What a fucking idiot this guy is." If you're in any of these categories, just skip this bit. Right now I'm talking to the person who is reading this thinking, "I want that, or some parts of that, and it feels like there's no way I can ever, ever have it." I want to validate that feeling. But I also need to tell you: you *can* have it.

You feel like you can't because that's the message we get when we're different. That's how the culture punishes people who are different: it tells us that if we don't make ourselves "normal," then we can't have the benefits "normal" people get. Family, friends, kids, work, and so on. That's bullshit. You can have them, even if it doesn't seem like it right now. I too was in your spot once, feeling alienated and lost and lonely and scared, ungainly and unlovable and ignorable and ignored, except as a target (and I had a metric crap-ton of privilege; I can't imagine what it's like to move through that place without). I can draw a direct line from that barren place to this fecund one, and so can you. You can. I can tell you two things I learned that might help.

One: Reach out, even if you're afraid. Work on activist projects. Go to conferences, which are full of people like you in some ways, whatever they are. Attend lectures and demonstrations and plays and concerts; they're free up at the university, and no one cares if you go there or ever went to college or not, so put that aside if you can. Lots of things have sliding scales or work-exchange. Ask people where they're going or where they've been if you're having trouble finding the right events, and keep asking and looking until you hit the right human or website or newspaper. If you're shy but in good respiratory health, go stand outside at intermission with the smokers. Don't smoke, because it's bad for you, but stand with them because the smokers are totally fine with falling into random conversation with whoever is standing around having a smoke. Go to meetings, even if it means taking three buses and ramen for lunch to do it. There is literally nothing that will encourage and excite you more than being around your people. Find a way, whatever it takes to do it, even if you feel like the most complicated, fucked-up being in the multiverse, because reaching out will show you that in fact you aren't. Not at all. You're another brave, scared person in a world of brave, scared people, and only people who are scared can be brave anyhow— bravery is feeling your fear and doing the hard thing anyway. Go be with your people, as much as you can. It will be so worth your while. Keep trying until you find people who really feel *right* to you; the ones you feel challenged and comforted by in just the right amounts.

Two: You're awesome. Don't let anyone ever tell you or convince you that they're the one doing you a favour hanging out with you, or dating you, or having sex with you. That's bad behaviour and you should have none of it. Be free of that noise and stay alone if you need to, or strategically on the margins, until you find the people who will adore you as you are. You may need to figure out a way to move, or change schools, or do something else different, but don't—really, don't—let people treat you like a charity case. You're a gift. Spend your time with people who know that.

Okay. There's more to come about parents and friends and hot times and hard times and my kid, too. Get yourself a treat, whatever you like (I am partial to a cookie, myself) and imagine that I am giving you a hug/kiss/queer nod/handshake/hand kiss/ thumbs up, which you can have in person if we ever meet at a show or reading. Take a break from the book if you need to. But come back. Please.

Are You Raising Him ... I Mean, Them ... Gender-Neutral?

A couple of years ago, when Stanley was quite small, there was a media firestorm that started in Toronto and blew across the world about a couple who declined to announce the genital arrangement of their child to strangers, believing this to be a satisfactory way to keep said child from being overwhelmed by people's expectations about how kids with that genital arrangement should behave.

It sounds peculiar when I put it like that, doesn't it? What could genital arrangement possibly have to do with what a person, even a small person, does in the world? And yet we are culturally obsessed by this—so much so that these very nice groovy parents with their totally adorable happy little longhaired children got all but hounded back into their house by the insane media attention and oversimplifying. What particularly gets me is that they never said anything more radical than, "We're trying to protect our smallest person from the cultural pressure around gendering, and here's our plan to do it." Meanwhile, all the yelling white guys on the TV started howling "child abuse!" I found this an especially interesting accusation coming from those who endorse spanking young children and hitting older ones with a belt, when "necessary." Declining to participate in gendered LEGO and rigidly pink/blue clothes shopping equals child abuse, but beating your kid with your bare hands does not. Good to know.

We sure do love our gendered categories, especially when it comes to children, and the wailing of "Won't somebody please think of the children!?" that religious fundamentalists and other agents of repression like to trot out rises to an especially fervent pitch when it comes to questions of children and gender. Especially gender-independent behaviour in children. So Kathy and David, who are quite nice and have three bright and healthy children, became Public Enemy Number One. This is even more hilarious once you know them in person, unless your idea of Public Enemy Number One is two cheerful people in colourful scarves who offer to share their homemade snacks with you at regular intervals. Eek.

Their youngest, Storm, is just about exactly a year younger than Stanley. When the story made headlines worldwide, suddenly, after never having heard a word about it, I started getting the same question—the question in the title of this chapter— over and over. More pointedly, people asked me why I referred to Stanley as *he* and *my son* when I didn't necessarily have that information yet, and what did that mean to me as a trans-identified person and educator? Did it mean that I didn't support my child if he ... if *they* ... wanted to live into some other gender?

It took me some doing to get comfortable with this question. I imagine part of my discomfort had to do with the accusation it came with—I'm never at my best when I'm feeling defensive and accused. But the larger part came as I questioned myself about it. Why *wasn't* I using gender-nonspecific pronouns for my son? Was I repressing his natural gender by referring to him as my son? Had I completely betrayed the cause of radical queerness and gender dis-essentialism as soon as I'd spawned, lulled into complacency by insipid children's music and the fumes in Babies R Us? People had warned me about this.

But let me tell you a little bit about my kid (a little bit more, I mean, than you have read so far). My son is currently, at the exact time I type this sentence, out with his auntie Abi—one of Ishai's longest and closest friends—attending an event at the High Park Zoo to celebrate the birthday of a llama named Dolly (I snickered too). He left the house wearing an outfit entirely of his choosing, to wit: pink-flowered sunglasses purchased this morning, a tan shirt with a huge blue monster baring its teeth appliquéd onto the front, purple and green corduroy pants with a bicycle screen-printed on them, green socks printed with a pattern of monkeys wearing DJ headphones, sensible Velcro-close Stride Rites in a wide width, and a slightly rusty silver clip in his blond ringlets. Over all of this, he's sporting a black coat made to look like a fire-fighter's turnouts. As he left, he was explaining enthusiastically to Abi that when they went to the big zoo he always had to walk really far, because he liked to see both the tigers and the lions, and the tigers live in the jungle but lions live on the savannah so they were really far apart at the zoo, and were there lions at this zoo too? And how far would they be from the llama? And would they be singing for the llama, and can llamas blow out birthday candles?

If that sounds adorable, it really is. If you're startled or skep-tical that a kid who's not yet three-and-a-half is discussing the respective habitats of lions and tigers, you've just never met Stanley in person. The overall effect is not unlike being knocked down by a little blond earthquake—it can be hard to focus on any single part of the experience the first few times. In time, though, one begins to be able to grasp all of what's going on. Since I started being asked about raising my kid gender-neutral, I have come to understand most of what goes on beneath the surface of the question. I think it mostly means, "If you're an expert about gender, then riddle me this: how do we best resist the forces of gender at our house, with our eventual (possibly theoretical) children or niecephews or whatever we have, for as long as possible?"

This is a legitimate concern. Once we know a kid's sex, we think we understand what they should wear, how they should behave, what they should like to play with, and so on. In short, we think we know how their gender should look. If you are someone who is worried about the forces of gender working on young people generally—pushing them toward some activities and away from others based on gender expectations, reinforcing a heterosexual future, narrowing their choices of clothing or hairstyle, and so on—then having an actual child of your own kicks this concern into overdrive. The very first thing anyone asks you when you say you're having a baby, or just had one, is: *boy or girl?*

Everywhere you go, everywhere you look, things are gendered and the *boy or girl* reductionist question just keeps coming. I had a really regrettable tantrum in front of a pharmacist's assistant a year ago when Stanley got lice. I went to get some of the special shampoo you have to use and when I said I needed children's lice shampoo, he asked, *boy or girl?* When I asked what possible difference that could make, he explained that girls would need a larger bottle to coat all of their hair, and boys could use the smaller one, because they have less hair. I pointed out that *boy or girl* was probably not then as useful a question as, "Does the child have long hair or short hair?" since—as he must know—there were sometimes known to be longhaired boys and shorthaired girls in the world. He replied by saying, "Whatever. Do you need it for a boy or a girl? I have a lot to do."

(There, in case it wasn't clear, is when the tantrum started.)

Baby clothes are terrible. Everything on the boys' side is blue and red and black or printed with cars or sporting equipment. All the shirts say ALLSTAR and GRANDPA'S MVP and #1 on them in Varsity font, and anything that's not adorned with a racing stripe has camouflage on it. The girl's clothes are all pink or purple or, uh, pink, and they all have rhinestones and glitter and a cap sleeve and a ruffle and a kitten on them. When Stanley asked for a purple shirt with flowers on it, it took a hilariously long time to find a purple T-shirt with flowers on it that didn't also have any embellishments deemed "itchy" (e.g., lacy trim, cut-out necklines, or shirred sides). And forever we were bringing home packs of innocuous-seeming onesies or sleepers only to discover that they had some message on them like "Mommy's hero" or "Grandma's flirt" in small print, just to be sure no hour might pass in a tender young life without a vigorous dose of gender-re-inforcing messaging.

Then comes everything else. Recommendations from the children's librarian? *Boy or girl.* Tiny bicycle, bouncy ball, backpack, socks? *Boy or girl.* The day I took Stanley to the store for a small-sized kid toilet he could use without needing a boost, I arrived to see the limited selection laid out for us with a certain grimness. He had been quite clear that he wanted the sort with a back and a "flush"-handle, just like the real thing (a stipulation to which I cheerfully conceded with visions of abolishing forever our cloth diaper pail dancing in my head). But when we got there, the only such items on display were from our friends at Pixar Studios: one red, Lightning McQueen, *Cars©*-branded potty with a stick-shift handle that revved for you when you pulled it, and one bubblegum-pink Princess potty adorned with moulded-plastic flowing skirts and a bejewelled sceptre that played a royal fanfare when you pulled it. My heart sank. Stanley ran to them, revving and fanfare-ing simultaneously, starting to declare his choices back and forth ("This one! Wait, this one! Wait ...") while I searched in vain for my alternative. A frog potty that briefly looked promising turned out not to have a back to it. I started to prepare to tell him we could look at another store when I saw, shining like a beacon in the sun, my salvation: Elmo.

"Look!" I shouted like I'd seen Bette Midler. "Elmo!" To my enormous relief, Stanley went for Elmo (who giggles and plays a flushing sound when you pull his handle). Crisis averted.

Keeping people from getting their gender expectations all over your kid is a full-time, elbows-out kind of a job. Our idea is that Stanley should get to wear and do and enjoy what he actually enjoys, regardless of who thinks it's appropriate for whatever gender they imagine him to have. Seems straightforward if you've never parented, but in fact it's an exhausting pursuit. Any commercial item—toothbrush, nightlight, bug spray, bath bubbles, even snack foods—gets printed with either a car or a princess on it. If you want an un-branded one, you're definitely paying more once you eventually find it. At any little kid's class or activity we've been to, the teacher or coach instructs and encourages the kids in gendered language—*Be strong like a king!* they say, or *Be graceful like a princess!* Our only respite was a circus class for little kids, where the instructor just asked them to straighten their backs like a ladder or to be limp and loose as a bowl of noodles. No imaginary regents necessary.

After a couple years of negotiating this, eleven times a day, simply refusing to say a word to anyone one way or the other about your kid's sex sounds pretty good. It sounds even better when you realize it means you don't have to spend any time receiving the unsolicited feedback of people who have had a thought they would like to share about your child's gender.

Ultimately, there are plenty of ways to raise a kid in a world of abundant, freely chosen gender. I respect and support the choice of Storm's parents to raise hir without publicly identifying hir gender as a way to make lots of room for that. Ishai and I, as two trans people with a lot of queerly gendered and trans-identified friends and family members, feel fairly certain that we will be able to make a space for Stanley where he knows he can wear what he likes and do what he likes without making a commitment to gender-neutral words, even if he hasn't yet asked to use them (to which, if he does, we'll cheerfully switch). Pronouns and gendered words aren't enough to constrain even a kid who knows the word savannah (he also said "cacophony" recently, and used it correctly. I mean, while I'm bragging).

In some measure, I think this question about gender neutrality also means: "Are you being true to your values about gender, even when it's your own kid on the line?" and to that I can easily answer yes. It feels fair for this to be a concern, and it's a valid one. Certainly, as a parent, there are days when I have to bite my back teeth together hard and take deep breaths in order to let Stanley give things a try. I'm proud of his fearlessness, even when it give me hives. So I think calming thoughts and watch him climb up things, jump off things, pour his own juice, and wear fourteen necklaces and a superhero cape out of the house. It's part of the parenting deal.

There are days when it take a lot of deep breaths to help me be as easy with gender-independence as my three-year-old. The day he requested the princess-patterned pull-ups I balked, I have to confess. My enthusiasm for gender-independence extends pretty far, but when it extends all the way into the hyper-feminine Disney realm of wasp-waisted whiteness, it makes my teeth grind. But our policy with regard to child raising is to say no only when we mean no, and then be unwavering in our noes, and I would only very strongly prefer he not choose things with princesses on them. I can't really bring myself to forbid it. I imagine there will be plenty of time for forbidding later, when he wants even more problematic (and expensive) things.

When Stanley came home this afternoon from his outing with his auntie Abi, he had in his hand a bag containing five rubber toy bugs representing the five stages of butterfly metamorphosis and was full of news about the llama, who turned out to be named Holly and who Stanley requests that he be allowed to invite to *his* birthday party in return, as seems only fair to him. He'd peed his pants, and returned home in his backup outfit: a powder blue baseball shirt with red sleeves emblazoned with the signature graphic from Abi's clothing design company, which reads "What's Your Mix?" in relief among the leaves of a complex and lush tree, along with grey pants and socks patterned with cupcakes. Although the shirt was originally intended to represent pride in being racially mixed, as Abi is, this kid's not afraid of his mix, either—his gender mix. Because of this, and also the bugs and the cupcake socks, the monster shirt and the pink sunglasses, I'm going to say that whatever relationship he has with gender, he's the one directing it for now, sometimes in a different direction than the last hour and sometimes in three places at once and sometimes nowhere at all, splashing and singing a little song about Alligator Pie quietly to himself. That—as far as his other dad and I are concerned—is as it should be.

Dear Parents
Who Have Written to Me

Dear Skyler's mom, Danny's mom, Evan's mom,
Laurel's dad, Scott's mom, April's mom,
and all the rest of you, too:

I'm glad you wrote. I'm sorry it took me so long to answer. I
have all this speaking and writing to do, even though I know
that's not an excuse. Also I have my own kid to handle, and he's
three now, and, well, I'm sure you remember three. Anyhow, it's
good you wrote anyway. I wish my parents had had someone to
write to—hell, some days I wish they did now. But let's just say I
get what you're going through.

I'm going to answer your questions as best I can and try not
to overlook anything. If there's anything else that arises, just ask
and I'll answer in my typically speedy way.

First: it's okay that you don't understand it. It's nice if you can,
and I encourage you to try if you're interested, but to be perfectly
honest with you, it's not actually key that you understand how
and/or why people are transsexual or transgender. We interact
every day with things that we don't understand, from the timing
of traffic lights to magnets to a cat's unerring ability to choose
the most important paperwork in the room on which to lay herself down. We might occasionally grouse or wonder about those

things, but we are also used to them and we can work with them. Same here. Trans people exist, your kid may indeed be one of us, and that is today's news. I would like to encourage you to let go of your need to understand for a little while, and focus instead on how you are going to love and support your child, which I assume is why you wrote to me.

Names. Let's talk about this thoroughly: it's unavoidable and it's complicated. I've named a child, so I understand how personal and hopeful and important a thing it is. I've also re-named myself, and I can tell you from being on both sides of the equation that it is just as hopeful and important on the re-naming end, and it is almost always undertaken—especially by people who are a little older—from a deeply yearning and often injured place. Naming, as you already know, is big stuff.

Our son Stanley is named for two of his grandfathers who were both named Stanley, and if he ever wants to change his name, I'll cry for sure. I adored my grandfather Stanley, and my husband Ishai did too, and there are days that I am so glad to have another Stanley Bergman in the world that it stills me. Your child probably wants a new name. I'm just going to say this, even though I know it's hard: you're going to have to get on board. It's just too hard to keep hearing a name that no longer feels like it describes you. My parents continue to resist calling me by my chosen name, twenty years later, and every iteration of my former name is like someone punched me in the stomach as hard as they could. I've had that experience. There's a moment when you feel like you'll never actually be able to draw breath again, followed by your dawning awareness of how very, very much it hurts, followed by a strong urge to vomit everywhere. You wouldn't actually punch your child in the stomach repeatedly (I'm assuming, but let's go with that), so you're going to have to get the name thing sorted out. It'll take time, but in under a year you'll be almost perfect—*if* you use it all the time. All the time. When your child is not in the room, say the new name anyhow. When you're talking to his/her/their great-aunt Petunia, at school, at church or mosque or synagogue, everywhere. Use it everywhere. If you only bother about it when your child is there to correct you, it takes a lot longer and everyone has a lot more hurt feelings.

I changed my name to Bear a long, long time ago, and I have worked and written and lived and loved and parented and done every other thing a grown person does under that name, a name I got when I was a teenager because I was very protective of my friends. Like a mama bear, they said, and started to call me Bear without any further discussion. I like that my name reflects my nature as a person, my best nature. The part of me that is also like a part of my parents, the part that goes to great lengths to take care of the people in my world (even if they made their own mess). My parents have never really been willing to call me by that name, and I never pressed it. I always assumed that in time, they'd get used to it—that they'd understand it wasn't my *nickname*, it was a name, and that I felt proud of it. That I felt named by it. But that day hasn't come yet.

Eventually, I changed my first name legally, in part because the Province of Ontario strongly discouraged me from changing my first name to just the letter S. I could have fought it, but I didn't really want to; it wasn't the S I was attached to but the history of it—being named for my great-grandfather, Samuel. But by the time it came to choose a first name that started with an S I knew we were going to have a new Samuel, my incipient nephew, and I didn't want to rain on Jeffrey and Lisa's naming plan. So I looked at names beginning with S that felt Jewish, and that described me—as I am—in some way that felt right. I decided against Simon and Simeon, seriously considered Shimon, and eventually settled on Sason, which means "gladness." *Kol sason v' kol simcha*—a voice of gladness and a voice of joy. I made a deal with myself that whenever anyone pronounced it incorrectly (as they often do), I could tell them when I corrected them that it means gladness. The general consensus is that it's a very good name for me, even if I don't use it very often. Bear's my legal middle name now, which also seems like the right choice.

But now this creates challenges. My parents know enough not to introduce me by a name I don't care for, but they don't introduce me by the name I have chosen. They just don't introduce me at all. And when they refer to me by my old name and as *she*, only people who have known me for at least twenty years have any real idea who they're talking about; when others figure it out, they judge my parents and disapprove of them for not using the right name for me, and they judge me and disapprove of me for not making them use the right name. These are not, generally, people who know my parents or they would understand, as I do, that it's not really possible to *make* them do anything. Which is why I haven't tried. I have just been waiting for them to understand for themselves that it's the right thing to do, and make the change. Like a punch in the gut, I tell you. Every time.

I don't actually mind that they sometimes refer to me as their daughter, strangely enough. It feels dissonant, but not untrue. I haven't been their son, and I am not certain that any off-season changes I may have made since my arrival into this world could make me a son, even though that's the word we generally use to refer to male children. I do not feel conflicted about being both a daughter and a father, or a daughter and a husband. They are part of my experience, and if I know anything about myself, it's that I am too enmeshed in my family to try rewriting my history in it, for good or ill.

(My brother, however, calls me by the right name and refers to me as his brother, which also seems perfectly correct. We've always been close and we still are—I'm pretty sure we'd be friends even if we weren't related—and he frequently takes on the supremely unenviable task of trying to introduce our parents to reason and good behaviour on the subject of my gender. Without my even asking him to. It really helps.)

Even still, I remain connected to my family of origin, partly because I am incredibly stubborn, partly because I now have a kid and want him to have a relationship with his grandparents, but also partly because I have a *very* positive, validating, happy life beyond them that they can't influence even if they disapprove of it. It's a pretty good life. I think it shows through in my work. I know this is one of your biggest fears as a parent of a trans kid. My parents were afraid, too. You probably don't know any grown transgender or transsexual people, especially if you're straight, and that makes it hard to imagine a happy future for your trans kid. That's what we do, as parents: we try to prime our little arrows to fly forward into the world. In all that time we're spending walking the floors with them while they're tiny and sitting up by their bedsides while they're sick and waiting up for them while they're teenagers and all the rest of it, we amuse ourselves by daydreaming about their futures. We picture them—tall and strong, smart and accomplished, partnered and with children of their own. So now, what your kid is telling you feels like it requires you to throw all those good hopes and dreams down the drain. It might even feel like they're saying they didn't want the care and time you were taking while you dreamed up those things. Not only that, you might not have any other futures to imagine, and so every attempt to picture your child's future ends in a giant question mark with awkward Chaz Bono-like facial hair and mostly the whole situation makes you feel afraid and helpless.

That's valid. It's an okay way to feel. It's not okay to act out your fear on your child, like my parents did—using force if necessary to make me do and wear feminine things because they thought if they could just make me more like what they thought of as normal, everything would be okay—but it is okay to be afraid. The thing is, there's not that much to be afraid about.

It's true, transgender and transsexual people sometimes face discrimination. It's also true that trans people who participate in survival street economies like sex work and the drug trade have a much, much higher rate of violence against them than those who are employed in other ways. But how do people end up participating in street economies? A primary way is that they're runaways or throw-away (kicked-out) youth. So the first thing you can do to improve your child's chance of having the happy and successful life you want for them is to keep them at home or safely housed with a relative or friend if for some reason home is impossible. And the second thing you can do is to start getting over your fears. I did say it's fine to have them. But I am also saying: then we move past them. Trans people can have great lives, great futures. We can be teachers and doctors and lawyers and veterinarians, city planners and machinists and writers and ship's mates, researchers and mail carriers and librarians and television personalities and assistant branch mangers—I personally know transsexual and transgender people who are employed in all of these careers. I also know trans-identified sex workers who are not doing survival work, but working in safe, supported conditions, and they too are well and doing fine.

I know that the popular culture seems to suggest that all trans folks are either niche performers on a Logo TV series or street-involved survival workers, but let's consider how the media works for a minute. Those are the stories that get people to buy papers. They're sensational. If a trans woman takes a job in Rahway, New Jersey, as an actuary and raises rabbits in her spare time, the media has no interest in her (unless, I suppose, she were to raise a really big rabbit, in which case her gender identity or surgical status would probably not be part of the story). I'm a transguy living in Toronto with my husband and our son and an old-lady black Lab, and if it weren't for the fact that I write and tell stories about queer and trans topics for a living, you would never have heard of me; I'd be a digital media manager for some groovy company, and you would only ever have read my name if you'd read my local theatre blog.

And yes—I am married. To a nice Jewish boy, no less (possibly not an issue for you, but of supreme importance to my parents). There are also plenty of people who are attracted to transsexual and transgender folks regardless of our various embodiments— some who like trans bodies, some who just don't find bodily topography a limiting factor, and some who find us so enthralling that they make exceptions to their usual sexual orientations in order to adore us up close in our skins. I also have a lot of really excellent friends, some of whom (but not all of whom) are also trans. Most of the things my personal friends and I do together are fairly nerdy pursuits like going to the theatre and taste-testing five different brands of mocha chip ice cream, but other people who are more outdoorsy than I am (so, everyone else, ever) play kickball and go hiking as well as doing the sort of grown-up stuff one eventually settles into: cocktails, dinners out, dessert, disco bowling. Our friends sometimes babysit our kid, or come over and bring their kids to play super-butterfly-trains with ours (they wear wings, they build train tracks, it seems absorbing and hardly anything ever gets broken. Don't ask me.) while the grownups have brunch. It's very urban, quite nice. We are all loved and loving, respectful and respected.

Not always, though. That's true. Indeed, I have been bullied and harassed. People have been unkind to me about my gender. I am pretty sure I've lost some job opportunities because of it. But the other, equally present truth is that nothing that has happened to me since I started living in the world in exactly the masculine, gentlemanly way I experience myself had been as bad as how I felt when I was still trying to hide, and when my parents were trying to force me to be more feminine. Because when shit has come down while I have been myself, I have dealt with it upright, in my full stride and authentic voice and with all the support and backing of my real friends and community behind me. I have been able to look back at them with honesty and honour in my words (even when I've also been scared enough to hear my blood pounding in my head), knowing that I am the one in the right. I've been scared, but I have understood always always always who in the situation was in the wrong and that it *was not me*. I have forged my courage in this embodiment, and I have grown it big enough to defend myself and a lot of other people with me. Whereas, before, it always felt like I was living in a lie—like any difficulty I might have been having was my fault and mine to sort out on my own, and that whatever support I had was conditional upon acting or being someone I wasn't.

Is it always easy? No. But nothing worth being is. And being true in the world has been invaluable beyond measure. It means I can devote my energy and time outside myself—to my work or family or friends or community.

Ultimately, your child is going to live into her or his identity one way or the other, and I hope it will be a luxuriantly long life they get to enjoy and not the kind tragically clipped short by despair. You can't change your kid, no matter what kinds of fears you have. What you're choosing now is whether you get to be the parent of "my folks were really supportive," or whether you're five years, ten at the most, away from "my parents and I don't really talk." Your children might turn out to be transsexual or transgender or genderqueer. Or they might be gay or lesbian or the other kind of queer or something else festive and new in the world of gender and/or sexual orientation. That part is not up to you. It wasn't up to you before they came out and it isn't up to you now, either. I know that's hard news, but it's the truth.

I also understand that it might seem like making them hide and pretend and lie is the right answer because they'll get less static in the world. It might seem safer in the short run. It might seem like a way of protecting your kid. But really, if you don't hear anything else, please hear this: that's how you make a kid ashamed of themselves. That's how kids get the message that their parents are ashamed of them and regret that they were born. A kid who gets bullied or taunted at school but feels loved and cherished at home (and gets to see positive images of other trans/gender-independent kids, of which there are many) will grow into a well and whole adult so much more often than a kid who fits in with peers at school but lives every minute feeling like they're an awful secret. That's also the truth. That's also the choice you're making right now. Please, please, choose well.

And if you're having trouble, please write back.

All best—
Bear

What Is It?

We discovered this morning that Stanley's passport expires a
week from Thursday. This kid gets a lot of use out of his passport,
having quite a bit of family in the US. Now it's almost Pesach.
His passport expires on the twenty-first, and Pesach begins on the
twenty-fourth. Oops.

So, in the realm of Dadly Tasks, there was one more to accom-
plish. I had to take him to get his passport photo. There's a place
nearish to our house where I've had mine done; the fellow who
runs it is a bit odd, but it's cheap and convenient. We go in and
explain what we want—actually, Stanley does; he is getting really
good about being able to politely and clearly address waitpeople
and counter staff (yet another thing that we are Working On). He
says, in his tea-kettle, preschooler voice: "I need my picture taken
for my passport." When I prompt him with a slight clearing of my
throat, he finishes: "Please." In reply, the proprietor says: "Okay,
young lady, come back here and we'll fix you right up."

Now. Stanley, for those few among you whom I've never forced
to audibly admire multiple photos of him, has long, gorgeous,
blond hair. Until he turned three, we kept it long because not
only did Stanley always have beautiful ringlets, but also because
Ishai enjoys esoteric Jewish traditions sometimes. Some Jews, by
custom, wait to cut any child's hair until they are three, to mark
the divide between the part of childhood where a child is only
responsible for soaking up all the love and attention in her or his

family and the part in which one begins to learn, participate in community life, and consider the needs of others. It's not terribly common in Canada, but that's never stopped us. Now, we keep it long because that's what he wants—we've offered him a haircut, and he has declined. He likes his long hair, and I am perfectly happy for him to keep it. It seems to result, fairly often, in him getting referred to as *young lady*, *little girl*, or sometimes *little miss*, but that seems also to be typically quite fine with Stanley. When we talk to him about gender—usually when he asks if a certain person is a boy or a girl—what we tell him is that some people are boys, and some people are girls, and some people are some of both. We tell him that everyone can choose for themselves what they want to be, and that we are a family that respects other people's choices.

Stanley often responds to this speech when we offer it by saying, "I'm a boy *and* a girl. But I am mostly a dragon. A middle-sized dragon."

So on this particular morning, as is the practice of our household, I do not attempt to "correct" the photographer about my son's genital arrangement or gender identity—also, as he's not here for a urology appointment, it seems irrelevant. But I guess I must have said something to Stanley, or addressed him in some way, which suggested to the proprietor that he was a boy child. I might have called him dude; I do that sometimes. I might have called him by his name. Honestly, that part's a bit of a blur, because of what happened next.

The photographer suddenly says, "That's a boy?" I reply, "That's Stanley." Stanley says, "I'm a dragon." His identity is very clear.

He sneers at Stanley and says, "That's not a boy. Not with all that hair. That's stupid."

I am starting to get a very bad feeling in the pit of my stomach, and I can feel my entire head starting to grow warm. I take a deep breath and before I can say much more, the photographer starts to shout: "That's a boy? No, it's not. What is it? What is it?"

He repeats his question—what is it? what is it?—several more times. I proceed to have a total loss of cabin pressure.

In retrospect, I do not remember very much of the next few minutes. I remember that I scooped Stanley up and held him very close, tight against my chest, to remind myself what hands are for. My instinctive response was to rip this guy's vocal cords out of his worthless throat and wear them out as hair ribbons (a.k.a., *not* what hands are for). At the very least, I was self-aware enough to understand that this was not a good choice. I shouted at him, at some length, and I am almost certain that there were expletives in the mix. I shouted at him until I felt my fragile self-control slipping even further and then, shaking and sweating, banged the door open as hard as I could and left. I put Stanley back in his car seat while trying not to either puke or cry, and *also* trying not to go back inside and scream some more.

While it was all happening, it feels worth mentioning, Stanley was perfectly calm in my arms. He displayed no fear, no upset that I was angry with him, no concern that he had done something wrong. Which logically makes sense to me (partly because he has never been spoken to in his life the way I spoke to the offending party). But, however, I also understand that proximity to loud anger can be hard on some people. He appeared—in the moment, and also later—to be very clear about who Papa was angry with, if not exactly why.

I drove around the corner and then pulled over and sat, breathing hard and trying to calm down. Stanley, from the backseat, asked me why I was so angry at that man. "He said something mean, sweetheart," I replied, shakily. "He was being mean, on purpose."

In saying it, I was able to understand that I was having a complete post-traumatic stress moment, that terrible experience of your entire rational mind splintering in a crash that sounds like a whole bar's worth of glasses and bottles coming down off the wall and onto a cement floor, shattering everywhere. I am frequently in places where "trigger warnings" are offered, designed to help people choose not to come in contact with upsetting content, but in my few experiences of being actually triggered, this is how it works. It's not content-based. It's not that someone is talking about something people find worrying. Everything is normal, and then the wrong phrase, or smell, or quality of light turns the world upside down; some fuckhead senior citizen starts saying "What is it?" in a gendered way, and meaning my very own personal child when he says it, and the world folds down to one reddish black halo around his face and it's every scrap of will I can summon to take two appropriate actions. One, do not kill him where he stands. Two, get child to safety.

I took deep breaths. I reached back into the back seat and put my hand on Stanley's calf, under the leg of his pants, so I could feel his warm skin, feel the realness and solidity of him. He was quiet, sucking his thumb meditatively, and I focused on the sound while I sat there, blowing and trembling like an overworked horse. Then Stanley asked, "What did he say that was mean, Papa?"

Oh, sweetheart. How can I explain this to you, when you have so little experience of meanness? When your whole frame of reference for the grave injustices of the world is that you are typically restricted to one episode of *The Muppet Show* at a time and are sometimes, non-consensually, covered with a blanket while you sleep? How do I talk about the historical impact of reducing a person to an *it*, and how this method of dehumanization has been used for centuries to enact unspeakable brutalities against so many groups of disempowered or disenfranchised people? Dear small person of such joy and trust, I am not ready to explain how our people were reduced to objects and slaughtered wholesale in so many periods of human history, and I am not ready to talk to you about my own very complicated relationship to being gendered as an *it*. I am not ready. I'm not.

I did explain, a little. I explained that the words he'd said and the feelings in his heart had been mean and unkind. I told him that sometimes, people who are very unhappy try to make other people unhappy. In particular, that they try to make others feel bad about themselves. Try to make us feel bad about ourselves. That man, I said, had spoken unkindly on purpose, and that was a very different sort of a thing from hurting someone's feelings by accident. I told him that we must always try very hard to speak kindly to others, because we did not *ever* want to hurt other people's feelings on purpose. I also told him that he hadn't done anything wrong, and I wasn't upset with him at all, to which he replied: "Yes, Papa, I know that." Well, all right then.

Then we went to a different store, because we still needed passport pictures, existential crisis or no. I was nervous, jangly, and on guard, and when we arrived and this photographer called Stanley "'little girl," I promptly replied, "He's a boy, actually," because if we were going to have a repeat performance, I wanted to know while I still had my jacket on, while I was still poised on the balls of my feet.

This photographer—bless him to seven generations—smiled. "Of course," he said, in the warmest tone. He told Stanley that he had beautiful hair and was very handsome, and opined that boys who look a bit like girls are always the most beautiful children. He knelt down and showed Stanley his camera and the chair in which he would sit, praised his good manners and intelligence, shook his hand solemnly, and told Stanley his full name—John Nguyen—when Stanley enthusiastically announced his own full name. John took a marvellous photo of Stanley and gave me extra copies besides, and when we thanked him he thanked us right back for coming in to see him and then said, after just a short pause: "He's wonderful. It's kids like him that make me want one of my own."

He looked hesitant, like maybe I would feel like he was over-sharing. But instead I gave him a big smile, and said, "Well, I really recommend it. You can't have this one, though. He's wanted." Then I prompted Stanley to say goodbye to Mister John, our new friend—which he did, because he is indeed very smart and quite well-mannered—and we left, waving goodbye behind us.

All day, I felt terrible. I felt terrible partly because we certainly contributed to his long-haired-boyness, and perhaps indirectly to today's wretchedness. But also, I was worried I'd upset him with my outburst. I posted a brief, bare-bones description of the morning's events to Facebook—there had been gender-policing, directed at Stanley, and I'd lost my temper at the offender—and spent the rest of the afternoon attempting to regain my grammar and good sense. When I checked back later, a flood of comments had come in, all suggesting some things I hadn't really credited: that it was good to have a parent who would stand up for him, that he would now know to push back against gender-policing. That I had done well. That Stanley was lucky, in this regard.

I am still breathing these ideas in. I am also still afraid about what may come for him, my tank-built, golden-ringletted, part-boy part-girl part-dragon. It's really true, what they say, about how having a child means letting your heart live outside your chest. This feels like a totally unsustainable situation, like a terrible trick; the sort of thing they really should warn you about better in those pre-natal classes. I did not need an hour's instruction on how to correctly wipe a tiny tush. I need to know how one stays at least as sane as one started out when now there's this person with awful discernment about risk and exceptional vulnerability in the world, who is also most worrisomely your favourite thing ever.

But then we picked him up from school that day. Where, we learned, Stanley had spent much of the day talking about how dragons can breathe fire *and* kind words too. Which is honestly so good an ending to this story I might well have made it up wholesale, if only I were as smart as my three-year-old.

What Are You Talking About?

When I was at school in Massachusetts, I had a friend who used to swear that she'd been switched at birth. She always felt she'd been born into the wrong family. The fourth of seven children and the daughter of staunch religious conservatives, she found herself, by the age of eleven or twelve, both questioning the religious tenets she'd been served with every meal since birth and able to understand and complete her much older siblings' homework in math and science. Wisely, she allowed her family to see only the latter of those developments, and she was sent away to school with us, a collection of smartypants at an arts-oriented school where we had such religious-sounding activities as Chapel three mornings a week (actually a fifteen-minute period in which one senior per day could say whatever they liked) and Vespers (actually a cultural event, usually a dance or musical performance). I think she coaxed her parents toward choosing our school by cleverly managing the information they saw and emphasizing things like 100-percent college admissions statistics, and that Caroline Kennedy went here too. So they let her come, to our little progressive groovy school where we founded the first ever Gay Straight Alliance anywhere, where we were divesting from South Africa, and where the headmaster hastily called a day of attendance amnesty on the day that George Bush, Sr. declared war in the Gulf because so many of us flooded into Boston to join the student protests. She fit right in at Concord Academy.

But when she went home, she found she had less and less to talk about with her family—even less than she had before, which was saying something. She couldn't discuss her thoughts about religion or politics, because her family would have found them blasphemous. Her courses at school were well above the education level of the rest of her family, and in the freedom of *in loco parentis* she had developed a range of hobbies and interests—from Hitchcock films to Ultimate Frisbee to eating dim sum in Boston's Chinatown—that she also couldn't talk about, not because they would be upsetting, but because her family didn't have any frame of reference for them. She still loved them, certainly, she just didn't have anything to say to them.

When we first met, when she first described this experience, I ... didn't really get it. I'd had disagreements with my family—they had been ongoing and in some cases brutal and certainly more and more frequent as I got older—but we never ran out of things to talk about, even if we were just continuing to fight about how I looked and what I wore and how fat I was and my complete failure to be sufficiently the girlchild my parents expected, at least it was a subject we held in common. Besides which, all my experience of the world was the same as my parents' experiences, more or less, or at least we had all these experiences in common since I'd been born. I had travelled only the worlds in which they had travelled. I didn't know anything they didn't also know. And for some people, that's the experience of their whole lives. They have roughly the same childhood their parents had, or they have the one their parents have created and mediated for them so they don't have to have the one their parents had. They worship together, they have similar social experiences; they go to the same college or an analogue of it, or they go to the same workplace or an analogue of it. They marry and spawn as their parents did. The parents remain more knowledgable and more sophisticated, at least about most things, than the child. We kind of expect a couple of breaks in this—technology and food being the most common ones, where the kid who was exposed to more things sooner becomes the parent's guide to Facebook or their iDevice or *japchae* or *sopapillas* or whatever "'newfangled" thing—but for a lot of people there's significant amount of overlap, significant experience in common.

Then I got exactly what she meant, because I came out. I came out at school, and I started to work with the Gay Straight Alliance and attend meetings at BAGLY, and then attend GSA retreats and speak to high-school students and teachers about being a wee queer and also meet adult lesbians and gays on America Online (this was before the World Wide Web, remember, when online services were private except for universities and the government) and on BBSs, and then meet them in person. There I was, all of six-teen years old, a wee tiny dyke with truly awful '80s hair, hanging around gay bars with a bunch of grown gay men in their twenties and thirties—a highly educational experience, but I certainly wasn't going to be discussing it with my parents. Once I forgot myself and tried to tell them a funny story that hinged on the listener having a working knowledge of the hanky code. Like most jokes, the more background explaining you have to do, the less funny it is, and the hanky code is entirely made up of gay sex acts (I was obviously out of my mind when I attempted this). There I was, trying to explain the hanky code and do a simultaneous translation into activities and behaviours that were *not* gay sex acts, and ... well. Yes. Suddenly, I had a flash of what my friend had been explaining.

(By the way, this was exactly as hilarious as you're imagining, once it was well in retrospect. In the moment, it was horrifying. *Horrifying*.)

As time passed, there were more and more things I couldn't discuss with my parents—not because they were predicated on knowing the difference between shrimping and felching, but because every new layer of understanding rested on an earlier one and they didn't have any of 'em. More and more, I found myself searching for conversational topics we had in common; less and less often did I want to share what was going on in my life—especially after I got blasted for "Everything being gay this, queer that, gay gay gay!" I flashed back to Harvey Fierstein's emotional appeal to his mother in the film *Torch Song Trilogy* (1988) after she accuses him of throwing it in her face. He replies to her, simply: "It's what I am." We could have been having this conversation at my house, complete with the Yiddish expletives that got cut between the play and the film, the yelling, and the slamming of doors. Needless to say, a gulf began to widen.

In reading about trans-racial adoption, where people (typically people of colour) are adopted by parents who do not share their racial identity (usually white people), I learned the term "cultural isolate." It's how they describe people whose family of origin doesn't share their ethnic or cultural identity. That's how it felt to me, increasingly, over time. If I wanted to interact with my parents, there was this chasm of understanding we had to span, and it typically fell to me to build the bridge because I was seen as the one who was "different" or "abnormal." They made it clear that I should bear the responsibility for this, largely by never attempting to bridge it themselves. So if we were going to share, I had to come equipped to explain whatever backstory there might be, weather any and all assorted uninformed or offensive remarks with good grace (lest I be branded "oversensitive"), and then do my sharing. As I'm sure you can imagine, I anticipated every opportunity for this with joy and delight. Or something.

This, it turns out, is one of the ways that relationships become brittle and difficult. There came a point when I simply couldn't saddle up for it anymore—not the explaining and definitely not the responses I got as payment for my hard work. I stopped sharing much of anything about my life, and started participating only in conversations about family members we had in common, where we should eat, and the weather. At one point I even started watching television again just so we'd have that. So every visit home became an exercise in figuring out what I could discuss that would be "normal" enough, while all my various news and projects and frustrations and triumphs—all of which occurred in my oh-so-queer life—piled up into a giant, precarious tower of unshared facts and feelings. Everybody knew it was there, and we picked our way around it—me, exhausted and my parents ... well, whatever they were. Possibly still living in hope that I was going to fall and hit my head on something and turn out to be heterosexual. And also pretty and slender and keen to fit in with the other girls. That happens, right?

I don't think either of my parents were aware of their own part in what was going on. Periodically I would get to suffer through a little sit down about being "distant and uncommunicative," which only made me less interested in visiting with them. For my part, although I could have told you that my parents didn't seem to have any enthusiasm for hearing about my life, I didn't understand the rest of it. Who does, when they're a teenager or a twenty-something? Only hindsight and a lot of reading have given me the part about cultural knowledge, or the part about what's Normal and what's Other and how we make up the difference. When we're young, we expect the grownups to do the heavy lifting, analysis-wise. Mostly, however, I think parents are often so soaked in The Way Things Are that they don't notice the root causes of this particular malaise. Me and my queer ways brought the problem, therefore we *were* the problem. End transmission.

This has been an issue with regard to many subjects, in so many cases that now, even when I certainly might choose to discuss any subject with my parents, often I don't have the energy to. I don't want to—for example—pause my grief narrative to educate them about why someone named Steve could have ovarian cancer (really, parents? After all this time?). So I just save it for a conversational opportunity with someone who can meet me at the point of conversation. After a while, the tonnage of what gets left out takes on the character of another entire force or being in the room with us, something hulking and silent. It's not really threatening, but as only one of the parties is able to acknowledge it for what it is, it's not reassuring, either. Sometimes I wonder what my parents think it is, this thing that's separates us.

I suspect they think it's my queerness, or maybe my gender. That uncomfortable thought leads me to what seems like the next logical question—for how many other families is this also true? How many parents or grandparents or family friends or caregivers in the world experience their queer kids as peculiarly distant or simply not forthcoming about their lives? How many of them blame it on the fact of a particular sexual orientation or gender identity? How many people involved in distinctly more radical politics or alternative sexuality or other out-of-mainstream pursuits have the same experience?

I recently attended a conference that presented, among others, a panel of sex workers who were discussing whether or how they were open with their families about their work and why. It broke my heart, listening to an entire panel of smart, thoughtful folks with various degrees of professional success explain that they didn't feel they could tell their parents about their work and that if they did so, their parents would likely no longer speak to them. One panellist had a nice-ish story about finding an ally in their stepmother, but otherwise the stories were grim. They were also familiar. Panellists shared their experiences of getting awards they couldn't tell their families about, becoming involved in legislative efforts they couldn't discuss, experiencing financial success they had to hide from their parents. They made up highly edited stories about their jobs, concerned that if they fabricated details they'd lose track of them, and so they contented themselves instead with stories of day jobs, former places of employment, and their less Google-able friends. One panellist began to cry, sharing that she was very close with her father and deeply wished to share her strategies and news with him but, fearing his disapproval, she hadn't yet made the leap. The panellists found, overall, that they couldn't see their families very much because of it, despite wanting to.

During the panel I found myself nodding often with empathy— both as a parent and as a child—though I wasn't quite able to notice why, yet. Afterward, in thinking about it all, I wondered: what does it take to bridge those gaps? While not usually an advocate of the "be a friend to your children" model of parenting, here's where I want my parents to behave as my friends do, and where I will behave as I have to my own friends when Stanley is old enough—I want them to take their own initiative to learn about what's important to me. In just the same way you might agree to try yoga with a friend who had dedicated herself to the practice of yoga, or research a particular form of cancer when a loved one has that cancer, or get a guide to Tanzania from the library when your close person gets a Peace Corps posting in Tanzania, I want parents—mine, yours, you yourself—to get themselves or yourselves to the library, or online, or into a group or even onto a Pride float (silver lamé thongs optional) if that's what it takes. The growing silence between me and my parents isn't caused by anything I've ever said about my gender or my sexuality. Ultimately, it's caused by what I don't say, because there's nowhere for it to land. If I felt like there was some context for it I might well choose to share quite a bit more. The pile of the unsaid would lessen. The shadow it casts would shrink. And in the resulting light, who knows what might grow?

I'm still not telling hanky code jokes, though. I only needed to learn that lesson once.

The Package Deal

I am never quite sure what to say when people ask how many children I have. That probably seems amusing, since there's very little possibility I could have gotten someone knocked up by accident, but it's the real truth. There's Stanley, who we made from scratch, who I've had since the beginning and written about extensively (sorry, kid); pretty much everyone with whom I've spent more than five minutes has heard about him (and seen photos and probably been subjected to a recitation of some recent cute or precocious thing he's said). We're definitely counting him as one. But fewer people have heard about Morgan, who is seventeen, and who came as a package with Ishai when I met him some years ago. I don't quite know how to talk about her, because how she is Ishai's is another complicated queerly familial story that makes him very like a parent to her, but also not quite a parent. They have the closeness an adult and child can have when the adult has been in the child's life, consistently and lovingly and in a workaday way since before the kid can remember, a please-get-the-trash, do-you-have-five-dollars-in-coins, love-you-too kind of closeness.

Then, after a whirlwind series of events unfolded in several states and provinces, Ishai and I took up together and with him came a very good dog, a metric ton of assorted outdoor gear, and this awesome energetic kid—Morgan. She's mine too now, even if the question of my *what* is a little unclear. My very beloved teenager, is what. My stepdaughter or my niece or The Household Teenager, she's mine and that's that. Typically, when asked, she refers to Ishai and me as her extra parents and sometimes she shorthands us to uncles, though most often she just calls us by our names because everyone with whom she spends any time knows who we are. We've picked them up or dropped them off, they've been to our house, and at the very least they've seen our comments on her Facebook wall (where I post articles I think may be of interest to teenagers that also seem to have something thoughtful or useful in them, because I know that, among her many virtues, she's also a tastemaker. My post will also get read by any number of other teenagers if it garners her imprimatur of satisfaction).

Morgan was eleven years old when we met, and at eleven she was too old for me to slip into her life while she was sleeping and wake up thinking I'd always been there, like they do with laying hens and small children. I had to rise and fall on my own merits with her, and if anything's ever been more intimidating than the preteen girl who adores your new beloved and has for her entire life, I don't know about it. Especially since my arrival came right on the heels of the disappearance of my predecessor in Ishai's life.

Interestingly, if she was ever suspicious of me, she didn't show it. I treated her first rather like a cat, not trying to ingratiate myself, just being with the two of them and letting my love of Ishai shine brightly through (not a difficult task, I will say). Later, she started a game of sassing me, picking on me teasingly to see if I would rise to the bait and get all authoritarian on her, a tactic I now understand as something of her trademark. She likes to see if adults hold their authority too tightly. I teased her right back, comfortably, familiarly, and for the first couple of years this was how we bonded—a running gag of mild insults. Since I come from a family where the appellation shit-for-brains is sometimes used as a term of endearment, this came easily to me, and in not-too-much-longer we had fallen into a solid fondness for each other. We share an affection for shopping, interesting accessories, musical theatre, and Ishai (and now Stanley), which stands us in good stead with one another.

But what does it mean, to claim her as my child? My step-daughter? I'm not wild about the *step* appellation when it comes to children anyhow. Naming a parent as a step seems like a sensible way to distinguish, if one winds up with a surfeit of parents, in which way and how long each of them have been in the picture. But adding the *step* to children always feels unkind to me, as if it's being invoked as a method of deniability: I got here late, don't blame me. I'm just the step-parent. I would actually prefer the opposite of that. If our notions of kinship and property and bloodlines valued time and energy a little more (and genetic contributions a little less), I would be happier, I think, generally. I embrace Morgan in all ways, in part because she has embraced me back so fully and so kindly, but I generally get on well with kids and am always happy to have them in my life. What I don't know how to negotiate is *un*-embracing them.

Let me be clear, it's not that I want to, now or ever. I do not think that we necessarily need to or must want to decouple ourselves from a romantic partner's entire family when the relationship ends, but often people get soured on each other and then the specifics get complicated. We ask our families to apply a transitive property to our intimate relationships. We present someone as the person with whom we intend to become a family, and sometimes this does not go how we hoped it would, and in the wake of this we find ourselves going back to those same family members and asking for lines of allegiance to be redrawn again. Once all hearts have been redistricted on paper (if not always in practice), forbidding forever the possibility that the former sweetheart can be re-elected, maintaining friendships starts to require diplomatic negotiations on the order of, "After everything he said to me, how can you have lunch with him!?" And so on. So I understand how these things sometimes happen—I just don't like it.

I used to have some other teenagers, besides Morgan. Two nephews and a niece, my ex-wife Nicole's sister's kids, whom I met when they were five, seven, and eight years old. Her family disapproved deeply of our queer relationship. I had hoped at least to be considered an upgrade after the previous several partners, for reasons I think most people would find valid, but I never really enjoyed anything more than a somewhat standoffish tolerance from her adult family (except her great-aunt Caroline, with whom I had an ongoing mutual adoration until her death). The kids, on the other hand, I really got along with—especially the boys, who loved my cool job working with UMass Athletics (and the never-ending free tickets to collegiate sporting events it provided) and my willingness to just sit and talk if they wanted to just sit and talk. We spent a lot of time together, especially over the latter five of the seven years Nicole and I were together, and our relationships blossomed to a place where they felt like they could call me when they needed things, sometimes. I was never happier than the day I got a call from one of them with a complex situation about some rumours and the bullying and various retributions that were accompanying them; we strategized on the phone for almost an hour until he felt some clarity about how he wanted to proceed.

And then, not long after that call, I saw all the kids—including the new little one—for the last time. I didn't know it was the last time, or I probably would have done a few things differently, but as it turned out that was the end of it. Beyond a certain day, my calls to their house went unanswered and unreturned. No one discussed with me that this would happen; Nicole and I were still in touch and even fairly friendly. We were sharing custody of a dog and a car at the time. But the split meant that no one was required to keep pretending to like me or approve of my relationship to Nicole, and ... the silence descended. I don't know if she requested it or if the kids' other adult relatives simply enforced it; it was technologically just a little too early for it to be easy to keep up with kids who were then twelve, fourteen and fifteen. Today we'd all be friends on Facebook and following each other's Tumblrs; the kids would probably all have cellphones as well—lines of communication are now more diffuse and far less easy to monitor. I don't mean to suggest that we would have snuck around keeping in touch in the face of a staunch parental directive against it, I only mean that's what it would take today to achieve the same kind of blackout. Eight years ago, it required only that no adult pick up when they saw my name on caller-ID (as the children were forbidden to answer telephone calls not specifically known to be for them after a debacle involving un-reported messages resulted in a grave misunderstanding and almost a felony), and that was it. I was out.

Of the many things for which I don't have a useful word, the process of becoming un-related to people—especially children—is about the saddest. Suddenly I was a revoked uncle, stripped of my privileges without even a chance to have anything to say for myself. If I hadn't also been handling quite a few other things,

I would have probably just gotten in my car and gone down there and turned up and waited, even just to say to the kids in person how they could reach me and that they were welcome to if they wanted to. That I did not want to be divorced from them, and hoped that they in time might rather not be divorced from me either. I refined this speech in my head over time, praising their devotion to their aunt, but also encouraging them to find me when or if they needed or wanted me without it needing to mean anything about my relationship to her. It was a great speech, but I never gave it. Paralyzed by a lot of emotion and upheaval, I never found myself ready to face the possible rejection inherent in such an appeal. There seemed every likelihood that they'd say No to my entreaties even if I was allowed to present them, which I doubted I would be. In the end I had to let them go like helium balloons, but without even the pleasure of watching them fly for a few minutes. They rose up and away from me, as children do and should, to new adventures about which I can know nothing. They were part of a package deal, and—though I was once in—I had been put out.

I wonder sometimes what would happen if Ishai and I ever found ourselves unable to continue. I don't feel like we're in danger of it, but I imagine people often wonder about that. It's my nature to worry and wonder and so I do, and one of my first worries is about the children—not just Stanley, but also Morgan. Legally I would have the right to half of Stanley's time, and I expect should that unhappy day come to pass, we would sort it out rather like that. But I have no right to Morgan, even if she weren't an adult now—no legitimate claim to her at all. She, too, could throw in her lot with Ishai as she would have every right to do, cleaving to him and away from me with her steadfastly loyal and loving heart. To some degree I'm counting on her intrinsic kindness to avoid that. To some degree I just don't care.

That's not right, it's not that I don't care. It's that I can't care—if I care, my only hope would be to try to protect myself against her eventual departure in some way, to harden my heart against her enough so that I might not experience any eventual dismissal as a catastrophic event. I won't do that. My instinct for self-preservation, which has never been particularly acute, is even more of a failure in this way than in most. I hear of people who learn to hedge their bets, who don't let themselves get too invested or too attached in other people. They set benchmarks and boundaries— not until the ten-year mark, not unless there's a wedding, only after the pre-nuptial agreement is notarized. That's all very well and good; I imagine it must cut down on the worry and also the weeping, but—it's not for me. As we all know perfectly well.

I miss my niece and nephews, but they came as part of a package deal. Sometimes a family is an all-or-nothing situation, and I came away from it with nothing in the family department. Here, with Morgan—and also in other ways and with other people, but especially with her—I am actively working to bind them into the family I have now. Even if protecting myself might ultimately make me less miserable, I still choose to be fully engaged. I'm giving myself to my relationship wholeheartedly in the hope that in the fullness of time I'll be part of Morgan's package deal—bearing and then forgetting her suitors in turn, letting my warmth or coolness to them rise and fall with hers. When or if they eventually fall out of her favour, they'll lose me too, and that is also part of the deal. In any given configuration, that's part of how we call someone family—we will turn away from those who harm them, even if it's difficult or inconvenient.

While I have both liked that fact very much and not liked it at all, I respect it all the same. Beyond that, now having thought this through thoroughly, I understand far more clearly why I resist referring to Morgan as my *step*daughter—because I don't want her to feel like I got saddled with her as part of the package deal. The word *"step"* somewhat unavoidably implies the distance between choosing and being presented with a *fait accompli*. I chose Morgan every step of the way (and many of those steps have been in clothing stores). I chose my niece and nephews, too. I keep choosing family—partly because by nature I am optimistic enough about love and connection to make a treefull of pink monkeys on nitrous look dour, but also because I want to be the kind of guy who always chooses family. Even now that I am old enough to know what that might someday mean, I want to be that guy. I have no disagreement with any of the other choices, but as for me, you'll find me in the third row of uncomfortable wooden seats at the eighth-grade orchestra concert (or analogue thereof) every time, smiling my face off and clapping my heart out. When people ask me which one is mine, I'll point like every other crazy-proud father and say, "That one, right there. That's my kid."

Inappropriate Intimacies

There are certain moments, usually when a particular song comes up as my iPod shuffles or sometimes during a particular type of news story on TV, when I find myself shivering with gratitude for some inappropriate intimacies.

Please let me be clear from the start: I'm not talking about sex. Sex is a way of being intimate, of course, but the two don't always go together (nor should they). Professionally, the euphemism around sex—the word that we're supposed to understand *means* sex—that upsets me most is "gender." They're not the same thing. And "gender" is a word we need to mean *gender*. But in my personal life, the one that's fundamentally most dispiriting is "intimacy," another word I need for its actual meaning. I am talking about actual, non-euphemistic intimacy. The sharing of confidences, of space, of emotional closeness; the kind of relationship that sometimes has a hush into which you can speak the whole and difficult truth. The way you can know someone in their socks.

Intimacy doesn't seem to be a popular topic outside of marriage self-help books, where it's a euphemism (again). From time to time, in discussions of cheating spouses, there's some discussion of intimacy as a version of cheating (called "emotional infidelity") and also as a compounding factor in an extramarital affair—was it a one-time thing? Or is this someone with whom the cheating partner has some sort of relationship? Prescriptions for these kind of inappropriate intimacies typically consist of advice like "cut all ties." The implication is that marriages only permit certain, approved kinds of intimacy to exist outside its boundaries, and that even non-sexual intimacy is suspect and dangerous. Partners would do well to beware, should they find themselves creating such a bond with a person to whom they are not married, if that person is of a sex to which they might be attracted. Intimacy, these books and lectures teach us, is a kind of gateway drug to infidelity, ruin, and regret.

This is why I wanted to be so clear from the beginning that this fond and grateful story isn't about sex. There was never, not even once, so much as an inappropriate touch or suggestion. But in each of the instances that were most present for me, most nurturing, most life-saving, I was very intimate friends with a much older, married or partnered, man who had some position of responsibility over me. Technically, it wasn't forbidden—how do you forbid a friendship that's too close?—but neither was it really permitted. We did it anyway and probably, without hyperbole, it saved my life. I can't say for sure that I mean that in the sense that these men were the difference between suicide or not, but part of why I don't know is that I had them (and they had me) (but not like that).

It's only in retrospect that I am able to understand how much of a risk they took; how scary it must have been in moments. At the time, when I was in my early teens to early twenties, I thought I was the equal or better of any adult in all ways. Closeness with adults felt satisfying. What I didn't really acknowledge—and couldn't until I was much older—was that I urgently needed to find grown men who would approve of me and treat me tenderly, since that was not available at home. My father and I were in the very long, very bad period in which the weight of his anger and disapproval hit me like bricks and felled me as quickly; I was hugely needy and hilariously arrogant. I try to forgive myself in retrospect for this and other juvenile offences, though it's hard to look back at cringe-worthy behaviour and sit with it comfortably. Or at all, really. Nevertheless, for whatever reason, there were those few people who saw something in me that they wished to nurture and took a chance to do it.

We sat together, a lot, mostly. In quiet corners of public places, with the doors open but with our postures closed—sitting together intently, with intention; I remember dozens of instances in which someone started to walk over, came to about ten feet away and turned back as though halted by a force field. There was a lot of question-asking and answering. There were a number of moments that felt distinctly dangerous to me, even then—dangerous and thrilling, to be taken into the confidence of a grown man. To be allowed into his interior, non-teacher, non-boss life; to hear his dreams and concerns and complaints. Understanding that I was having a completely different experience of him than the other students or the other employees was almost as satisfying as being able to share and feel—it meant I was *worthwhile*. Or at least, that's what it meant to me at the time, in stark contrast to the message I was getting from my father that I was unlovable and always would be (until, or unless, I became a very different kind of person). I'd been chosen for something.

Through time's ease I think I understand that all of them felt the lack of intimacy in their own lives too, in different ways. They must have, to have felt ready to meet me in the intractably needy place from which I reached out for them, hungry as a baby bird for any amount of affirmation that I was worthwhile, valid, desirable in any regard. They must have, to be willing to take the risk that came with it—of a young girl/young woman, as I was then, being near or sweet with them. The uproar over inappropriate relationships is sharper and more present now than it was in the late eighties and mid-nineties, but it existed then too. There were wives to consider besides which, with two of them. Even still, I was permitted. Young me, girl me, wanting and unsubtle me, I was allowed into their intimacy.

I could not recount for you any one single conversation or moment that felt like the beginning of it. I'm not sure how it happened or what signalled the change or when I understood what was going on. I could if I played it back now, I'm sure, but not then, not anymore than a starving person could discuss with you the seasoning of the soup. But somehow slowly I was in, inside with each of them, inside in a way that felt far more intimate than I knew I should be allowed. I swam in their thoughts about their work and love and children, their frustrations and discontents, their childhood stories. I considered them. We discussed them. I'm sure I gave inappropriately reductive advice. I listened a lot. It may actually be the case that I finally learned how to listen, in those relationships.

Always I yearned for more, though I wasn't ever quite clear about what "more" might look like. We were already beyond the bounds of propriety, but constrained within our roles as teacher/student and boss/employee, twenty-year age gaps snapping between us. I liked it that they were willing to risk something for me—I have to be honest and acknowledge that I liked it a lot—and also I wasn't satisfied with it. In my imagination, there was some different thing yet we could do, or be, that wasn't confined to office hours and daylight chats on camp or campus benches, even if it wasn't sex I wanted. What I think I wanted was for the intimacy to feel boundless, to twine ourselves together even more closely, as you do during long road trips or encounter weekends, during the times that time stops meaning much. When what's counted isn't minutes but breaths, meals, secrets. Maybe you've dropped into that space with someone before, beyond the cares of the world. It often happens at night, which might be the thing I wanted that felt like more—that out-of-time feeling.

Nevertheless, I got a lot. As time passes, I feel more and more grateful for it and more and more surprised that it was available at all, that several different people took the time and trust to be intimate with me in ways that would almost certainly have gotten them censured if anyone in a position of power had understood the depth of connection. Not because we were doing anything wrong, but because many other people might well have, you see? In an institution, that's not allowed. The line of propriety is kept well back from the actual line of transgression, like a moat, so that movement toward transgression can be spotted and arrested. Except that we weren't, as far as I know. Not in any case.

I have been in and out of communication with these men since circumstances moved us out of each other's physical orbits. In all cases, I have had a hard time separating and also in all cases, I thought I was the only one who was having a hard time with the separation. I don't know why, even after giving it long thought. Maybe it always seemed like charity, in some way. But the reality, after a few years' break, that each of them missed me or longed for the return of that intimacy was almost as startling as the fact it existed in the first place. Maybe more, because I can see in life's rearview mirror what I was like then, and I don't know if I could have liked younger-me enough to miss me. I must have been all right somehow, though, because they did and do. They're proud of me and my accomplishments, and of our closeness and the parts they played in my development and thinking. I'm so grateful to be able to return that, after the chance they took on me. It's a little easier since I'm grown now; we can have coffee when I can get myself to their various far-flung cities to spend a little time and talk. I think we could stay out all night now, but I wonder whether something would be ruined if we did.

I read a line once, I'm fairly sure in one of Armistead Maupin's novels but could have been John Preston's non-fiction—a wistful, post-AIDS reminiscence of "falling in love on any afternoon for five minutes at a time." As I've gotten older and had more ways of seeking intimacy available to me, I have chosen to pursue most of them in some way. Many of them have been lovely, restorative, and nurturing, and some have been a world of hurt and grief, which is the price you pay when you bring your heart to things. Intimacy is the word I would use instead of the phrase "falling in love"; I think falling in love takes quite a bit longer but intimacy can open fast and deep (if narrow) like a canyon you fall into together. But there's love either way, isn't there?

Love is a word I haven't used yet in all these couple thousand words about intimacy; still afraid to get someone in trouble, I guess. *Inappropriate love* sounds even more suspect than *inappropriate intimacy*, but what I had was both. In all instances, it was both. People accused me of having crushes sometimes, or sometimes of sucking up or playing teacher's pet. None of which were right, but I couldn't very well defend myself by saying, "I don't have a crush on him, we just love each other."

But we did. We knew each other, and we tended to each other, and we loved each other. We shouldn't have been able to; it wasn't allowed, and we did it anyway and it very probably saved my life.

Maybe it gave me a life I wanted to stay in. For sure it showed me something about life and gave me a taste of what I could look forward to in the world that existed outside the confines of my own miserable circumstances. For sure it made me feel as though I could be lovable and helped me to feel as though some other person might well someday love me in a more "appropriate" way. But like other similar things—like fire and language—we handled it respectfully and were therefore sustained by it.

Gay Married

It's the comedian Wanda Sykes who quips, "I recently got gay married or, as I like to call it, married. I don't have gay lunch, I have lunch. I park my car, I don't gay-park it." The bit usually gets a big laugh from straight supporters of the marriage equality movement, and sometimes from married gays and lesbians. Indeed, they are getting Married, and they want everything that comes with that, I think—not just the opportunity to kit out their friends in funny colours and register for a coordinated set of Le Creuset cookware (oh, and the inheritance and hospital visitation rights), but the sense of fixed-ness. The odour of respectability that comes with it seems just as satisfying as the tax breaks; where heterosexuals can afford to casually disdain marriage even while they cohabitate and spawn, queers are not assumed to be especially serious about one another these days if we don't get ourselves hitched.

For the record, I am hitched. Or, to be specific, I am gay hitched. Not just in the sense of general-duty fabulousness in evidence at our wedding, which was not inconsiderable, but also because I do, really, believe that I have gotten gay married, and that this is a different and queerer thing than the other kind.

My gay marriage is not, for example, sexually monogamous, a condition which seems to be the default of straight relationships and wasn't of queer ones for quite some time (though, certainly, some people always chose it and no one really blamed them; it's a harmless perversion). If it seems odd that I write that in a book about family, if you find it jarring to read sexually explicit work in this and other books of mine right alongside tender, meditative paeans to making or parenting my small son, I would encourage you to ask yourself: why? Do you imagine that parents don't have sex? The worldwide preponderance of younger siblings seems to betray the lie in that thinking (though I will admit it takes a little doing during that first infant year). I think it's something else—I think it's the way that the heterosexualized marriage imperative has made us think differently about grown-up relationships, even between two queers, especially if they have children.

Children, I am here to tell you, are not the end of sex (and only sometimes are they the result of it). And marriage is not the end of sex, either, and neither is monogamy, for that matter (or so I hear). But we're so conditioned to hide and erase our sexual desire as somehow damaging—to The Cause if we're queer or trans, to The Children if we're parents—that we get silenced into acting like it is. We fear punishment of various kinds, from social tsk-ing to the very real and utterly terrifying interest of the state in our children's welfare if we don't comply with the sexual silence mandate.

(To be clear—I believe sex and sexual exploration are profoundly human activities that should be pursued with our enthusiastic consent and with people we choose, who choose us back, in age-appropriate ways. And I'm upset to the point of rage-nausea when I hear about the rape or sexual abuse of children. But I am also profoundly annoyed that I have to stop and say this explicitly in the middle of an essay that's otherwise flowing pretty well because I have good reason to be afraid of what might happen if I don't. I'm self-policing a little so I can get away with transgressing in a different place, if the reader will kindly take note.)

And so being gay married, or queerly married, leaves room,

in the same way that I once heard someone described as "San Francisco monogamous"—the person in question made porn and the couple sometimes pursued a third person together, but all *other* sexual contacts outside the relationship were forbidden. Being gay married leaves space for things that married simply does not, and one of them is to make our own decisions about sexual monogamy. During the process of application for my residency in Canada, Ishai and I decided on governmental recognition of our intensely romantic proclivities in part because applying as a common-law, unmarried couple meant swearing sexual monogamy on the application form. Married people were not required to swear this, presumably having made our promises somewhere before the notary's office, and so we went for the full marriage option where, in other circumstances, we might just have had a religious ceremony and left the other business out of it entirely.

Being gay married also leaves us out of presumed, hetero-style gendered divisions of labour. We both work at things; he in the school system and me thinking and writing and hustling one-off work out of universities, and we collaborate on the full-time raising of a highly energetic and terrifically curious small child. The nature of the household collaboration is that most duties are shared—by time, if not by instance (that is, we each fix a meal a somewhat equal number of times, not that we squeeze ourselves into the small kitchen together and attempt to co-cook). A few things are Balkanized by personal preference and proclivities. For example, I do all the household shopping, including every-one's clothes and shoes, because I am good at it and Ishai hates it; Ishai handles the household finances because he's good at it and I hate it.

But otherwise, we share. We make chore plans—dog walk,

breakfast cookery, kid dropoff and pickup, dinner, bedtime tasks—
for the day based on energy and schedule and fondness, because
we can both do everything. We have a household rule that goes,
"If you did it, you did it right," designed to prevent anyone com-
plaining about how anyone else completed a chore, and this is
wholly a part of the family fabric across all areas now. You'll never
hear any of the adults in our house griping that the dishwasher is
loaded incorrectly or the socks are not paired "right." (Feel free to
steal.) I have the clearest memory of reading a book called *Equally
Shared Parenting* in which the authors championed the idea that
both parents should know how to do everything their child might
need, and finding it ... puzzling. The book had come with so much
hype. Revolutionary! Profoundly Feminist! And so forth. But we
were six or eight months into being the parents of a three-dimen-
sional, exterior baby at that stage and nothing contained within
the book seemed even remotely like new news.

Well, yes. Both parents would do anything a child could
need. What would the alternative be? Leaving a wailing infant
unchanged or unfed or un-soothed? Evidently, yes. I'd been so
removed from the parenting and coupledom narratives of hetero-
sexuality that I'd completely forgotten about the phenomenon of
fathers absenting themselves from the proceedings on the basis of
ineptitude. Not only that, but I certainly had seen my own father—a lifetime baby-stealer—feed and change and soothe infants
all the time, even those belonging to other unrelated people, while
singing nonsense songs to them. I didn't get it that when there's
a mom and a dad in the deal, dads often get excused from knowing who is due for a doctor's appointment or what size shoes or
clothes anyone wears or which child prefers what vegetable or
preparation of their toast. Being gay married also comes with gay

parenting, where we both know where the vaccination records are, and that Stanley wears an 8.5 wide shoe, and likes his toast cut in triangles or soldiers and the crust left on (we have systematically and vigilantly erased from his landscape the idea of crusts being cut off the way some families erase the existence of queer people. It is Not Spoken Of).

Gaily married as we are, we can also make these decisions without having to defend them to anyone. There are no expectations of what a couple of the same sex will each do in the giant matrix of chores that is daily life or parenting. "Who cooks?" was the question my grandmother's generation asked of queer couples as a way of trying to map some gendered roles onto an unparseable reality. But whether the answer was Bruce or David, Lynn or Carole, no one was surprised about it—not in the way that people are still startled when hearing of straight couples in which the man does the regular, daily, dinner-on-the-table cooking. We do not expect that in a capital M, un-adjectivized Marriage.

It has not been lost on me that cries of "smash the family" are based on a gendered, rigid, exclusive model of marriage—the classic, your-father's-Oldsmobile variety, the one that so many straight couples pretend to practice even though their interior realities are often so different. I sympathize, though—when the trajectory of your life is so narrowly laid, and no one around you reports any active discomfort with it, and divorce is seen as a broken instance and not a broken system—well? How could they know they can make their own marriage rules, or even see the evidence that this is even an option?

The cost to all this imaginative freedom is queerly familiar as well—I am gay married, and not just plain married, because my gay marriage is so frequently questioned as to its legitimacy. Gay married also means "void where prohibited by law." Every time I cross, with my husband and our son, into the United States to see my relatives there, I am reminded of this because only sometimes are we recognized by the Department of Homeland Security (a phrase for which there cannot be enough air quotes) as a family. Half the time one or the other of us gets sent back to visit a different wicket, because the policy of the United States Government is that queers can't get married. So for a while there I was gay married to my husband in Connecticut where my parents live, but legally a stranger to my husband in New York where my brother, sister-in-law, and nephews live. It was dizzying. We made fun of the situation, but it was distinctly a gallows humour.

We base our travel decisions on where we think our family will be safest if something were to, G-d forbid, happen, our childcare decisions on which school seems ready to make curricular room for a two-dad parental set, and our choice of synagogue, ditto. The synagogue my husband loved best as a single guy and would have ideally joined would not have us as a family—they don't recognize us as Married, even if the province of Ontario does.

Which is profoundly demoralizing. Even though I know, and can make, plenty of arguments about why the marriage equality movement is troubling and how we could have spent that money better and the perils of relying on state sanctions—these are all logical arguments. A logical argument, no matter how sharp, no matter how flawless, will never trump an emotional argument. And the gut-punch of being required, by uniformed individuals carrying firearms, to un-marry ourselves upon their instruction in order to enter the United States of America is as emotional an argument as I know.

That's what being gay married looks like—your marriage is

provisional, easily revoked, or undermined based on context or whim. In this way, it is profoundly unlike Marriage. Straight people's marriages, whether performed by a tipsy Elvis impersonator or the Archbishop of New York or your best friend from camp who registered to be an officiant on the Internet, are equally recognized and legitimate. They're legitimate no matter the age difference, no matter how long the parties have known one another, and nowadays regardless of the racial or ethnic backgrounds of the bride and groom (a situation too long to come, indeed). When I tell people from the US that I am married to my husband, their first question is often: "Is that legal?"

(I have been known to quip, "It's only a misdemeanour charge if they catch you, so we decided to risk it." Tellingly, at least a couple of folks out of every ten believe me.)

So, with apologies to Wanda Sykes, who is trying to both get a laugh and make a point, I can't agree. It's true that I don't gay park my car. Whether any of my lunches has been gay may be debatable, considering that that I frequently have lunch meetings at Toronto's LGBTQ community centre, and also that I hold my pinky finger up when I drink, and *also* also that at least one of my lunches led to the one-night stand that became a weekend fling that became my gay marriage.

But my marriage? Gay as a box of birds. And honestly, on balance, I wouldn't have it any other way.

How to Keep Your Man Happy

I am hunched over my computer at 4:30 in the morning, which is 9:30 in the morning in Scotland, having set an alarm and sneaked out of bed to catch the end of this eBay auction. I don't think it's going to be a problem, snagging this treasure, but it's for my husband's birthday and I feel the need to babysit it, to be absolutely sure I'm not edged out at the last minute for fifty pence. The seconds count down on my screen but there are no other bidders. I win. I sit back, delighted, and scroll again through the photos of the item I believe will be the perfect birthday gift for my man: a covered vegetable tureen.

Not just any tureen. A Mason's Regency Plantation-patterned tureen, edged *and* scalloped, in a bright four-colour floral pattern with a snail luxuriating among the blossoms. The same pattern as his Granny Charlotte had; the same pattern as all the dishes in our kitchen are now, hand-carried back from the village of Wetheral in Granda Stan's old leather suitcase in the summer after the both had passed. The dishes are, in a Yiddish word, *ongepotchket*. "Excessively decorated," is the English translation of the word, but it doesn't quite convey the whiff of excess that the Yiddish does.

And for the record, let me say: when it comes to housewares—especially the kitchen—I am of the nautical variety. I like plain, clean lines, the sort of dishes and furniture that designers continue to describe as "masculine" for no good reason. I like metal, wood, and stone. All previous dishes in my entire life—not just the ones I have chosen, but the ones my parents had when I was small and those they have now—have been variations on a theme of white-with-one-blue-stripe. For a while around the turn of the century, they used a set that was white with two asymmetrical blue stripes, one wide and one narrow. You could tell my parents found this tremendously daring.

I like things that are white with one blue stripe. I think books are decorative. I like battered old baskets and chopping bowls, my great-grandmother's silver pitchers, and on the wall the pornographic 300-year-old Japanese prints my brother the art dealer got us as a wedding gift. Otherwise, I am hardwood floors, Imperial pint glasses, white bathrobes, and wood boxes. I am not hand-painted dishes, riotous with flowers and snails and scalloped edges.

But my husband is. His grandmother was, and his love for her and his grandfather wends its way through his universe, and now mine. He remembers eating so many of the happy meals of his childhood off these dishes. He felt loved and cared for and fussed over on these dishes; this is the china pattern upon which his favourite foods were served just for him, in the farm kitchen next to the AGA in the way far north of England. He holds the one crazed and browned plate with extra care, the one his granny used to keep in the oven with lunch still warm on it until his Granda Stan came in from the fields, even though the cheese plate and the mustard pot and certainly the teacups would fetch a great deal more at auction.

When his granny passed, he asked his mum to pack up Granny's dishes and save them for him. She, being a practical sort, packed up eight plates and the six matching bowls. She packed them well in layers of newspaper, tied them securely into a box edged all around in bubble wrap, and then left all the other odds and ends on the shelves. When we arrived almost a year after, to visit that branch of Ishai's family, my husband packed up every last shard of dish in the precious pattern and we brought all the dishes back (the transit itself a hilarious story but one that requires the visuals; ask me at a show sometime). And then my job began.

When we got it all home and sorted it out, we had a lot of plates and hardly any bowls. I thought, well, I'll just go online and pick up a few, then, shall I? And my sweetheart will be so pleased. From time to time on a special occasion we'll pull them out and have breakfast on them, and he'll be happy and, because I love him so, this will make me happy, too.

Best laid plans, et cetera. I bought the bowls, and the dishes started to look like a full set. They went onto the shelves. I noticed that more and more often I reached for them when I was plating food, and I kept looking for further pieces—a cake plate, a serving bowl, a set of soup plates with broad rims for balancing a piece of bread upon. I liked the days that the parcels in their coated brown-paper wrappings would arrive from the United Kingdom, airmail, addressed to my husband, and I could casually set them on his desk and walk away feeling pleased.

I was the one who eventually suggested getting rid of the old, plain navy dishes and installed all of Granny Charlotte's on the shelves. I was also the one who, when we got pregnant, started quietly buying extras of things we already had enough of with the expectation of youthful breakage. Ishai looks so happy when they arrive, it's like the reverse of Post-Traumatic Stress Disorder. The very pattern seems to be a happiness trigger. He greets every new item with an intense, if quiet, pleasure and carries it carefully into the kitchen to sit on the shelves beside its spectacularly overdressed siblings, of which there are many. We now have platters and mustard pots and vegetable dishes and even a ginger jar and a toothpick holder. The first use of each is an occasion of ceremony, and we welcome it back among its brethren.

This morning, the tureen—and therefore a happy birthday—are assured. I climb back under the warm covers and snuggle in beside him again; when he stirs, I lie to him and say I've been having a pee. But I haven't been. I have been up loving him across years and continents and design sensibilities, imagining as I click how much more I will enjoy a plate of buttered early peas when they've been served out of a tureen that lights him to the toes with joy.

Especially, I think as I drift off, if I can find that matching ladle somewhere.

Machatunim

As a teenager and twentysomething, making my annual visit to my grandparents' in Florida (where Jews, as we know, go to retire—both sets of mine did), I followed two rules, developed over time. They invariably made my trip easier.

Rule one was to be absolutely sure that I was staying for an odd—not even, but odd—number of meals. This meant that neither grandmother could claim that I favoured her cooking or company over the other grandmother's during their subtle jousting sessions. And when I say subtle, I mean, you know, contextually. There's a reason that "subtle as a New York Jewish grandmother" is not a well-known phrase. Odd number of meals meant that I could eat an exactly equal number of meals per household, plus one to meet in the middle for the event that my family—for reasons probably better left unexplored—has always referred to as "prisoner exchange." There we'd be, me (giant queer grandchild) and my four shrinking grandparents, having soup and salads for lunch. At eleven a.m. It wasn't really pleasurable in the classic sense of the word, but it was worthwhile. And evening out the meals eased the way a little.

The second rule was to go first to my mother's parents, and then to my father's. My maternal grandparents, Nana and Pops, were the country-club, golf-tennis-bridge sort of retirees. They ate several times a week in the big, fancy country-club dining room, a temple to tennis whites and golf skorts and slim midriffs on senior citizens. Visiting grandchildren obviously meant a dinner in the club dining room to show them off, and a further round of friends invited to "drop by" to "say hello"—a non-subtle way of saying, "My grandkid came to visit me. Ha ha."

This meant approximately 100 million iterations of the same awkward conversation—from thirteen to twenty-two, it was a conversation about whether I had a boyfriend yet, and from twenty-two until, oh, say ... say, yesterday it was a conversation about whether I was my brother. All of these conversations had to happen at maximum volume ("Wait, who are you again now, dear!?"), and with people who would proceed to bust out photos of *their* granddaughters at any opportunity. Their granddaughters were all slim and pretty. And did indeed have boyfriends. And were also, you know, still girls.

Ahem.

At the home of my other grandparents, however—my father's parents, my grandma and grandpa—what we did was mostly eat, read, and talk. It was a little more ... my speed. And I discovered that if I did the country-club business first and then the eat-read-tell stories part after, I returned to my regularly scheduled life in reasonably good spirits, despite having eaten dinner at 4:30 p.m. for a week running and not having had ten seconds alone time.

My grandma, particularly, enjoyed a good argument. Also Miami Heat basketball and political fiction. She loved puns, word games, and crossword puzzles, and loathed George W. Bush. Loathed him so much that sometimes we'd just sit around and take the piss out of him.

So when last week I got a call to say that her aide had arrived Monday morning to find her barricaded in her apartment, screaming and crying and cutting up pictures, unable to recall the names of anyone in the photos or remember how she knew them, I knew immediately what I wanted to do—and it wasn't anything I'd ever have expected to be the answer. I wanted to call my friend Ivan.

Ivan is also a storyteller, also a bit of a travelling circus, also a tender-hearted kind of a fella who has chosen to stay enmeshed with her family even when they drive her batshit. Ivan is also sweet on her grandmothers—the one still living and the one passed—in much the same postcards-from-anywhere-interesting-and-phone-every-Sunday way that I am. We've toured together quite a bit, talked about our families both onstage and off, and poked fun at each other in a variety of states and provinces. Ivan has thirty-five more first cousins than I do, but we don't let that sort of thing stand in the way of a solid working friendship.

My brother and I are the only grandchildren of this grandmother, Rita Fergenson Bergman, born in 1919 and as of this writing age ninety-two. You'd think he'd be the one I wanted to call. Especially because I am so fond of him—seriously, he's the awesomest straight guy ever. Ivan's never eaten my grandma's stuffed cabbage (though I can confidently predict she would have loved it) and my brother has, a million times, and he knows her funny foibles and expressions, like how she calls her regular indoor glasses her "white glasses" to distinguish them from her sunglasses, and the way she used to send us letters at camp and then later at college, enclosing crisp bills and exhorting us to go "buy a stick of gum" with them.

As I think about it now, I realize that as the bills got larger, the things we were encouraged to buy got smaller. When it was a five, she said to get an ice cream cone or a new book. But with a fifty, I was told to buy a hair ribbon, and my brother a baseball

card—long after either of us purchased those things. She's a joke-
ster, my grandma.

She was. That's how you knew she was in good spirits. She'd
make utterly ridiculous jokes about your abilities, her own, or
someone else's. On the opening day of baseball season, she'd say
she was waiting for her call to go play for the Marlins, and when
our son was born weighing over ten pounds and a great squalling
chunk of good health, she asked, upon seeing the photos of him
at three days old, if he was driving yet.

I didn't call Ivan that day, because I knew I'd cry, and I couldn't
quite figure out how to call her up and say, there's a problem with
my grandma, do you have a little time to listen to me blubber
into the phone? Which she would have, no doubt. Ivan's spent
as many hundred hours sitting across an old table from a smart
old lady as I have, coaxing the stories out of her, filing them away,
taking her to do her shopping, carrying the heavy stuff, holding
the door open in a queer-granddaughter kind of way that still
feels gentlemanly even to someone who changed your diapers
and does not see you as any kind of man.

When her little gran, Florence, passed two summers ago, Ivan
talked and told stories about her for months; I got three different
phone calls that summer that started out to be about business and
ended up to be about her gran. My husband and I had just gotten
married, and he was pregnant with our son. Ivan and I talked a
lot about our families all summer long, and in the late fall, too,
when we went on tour down the West Coast and each night the
onstage patter deepened into a cyclical groove of celebration—her
little gran, just passed and my son, soon to come. We made audiences cry from San Francisco to Victoria, BC, telling all kinds of
family stories—butch and femme and trans and queer, blood and

marriage and not-marriage-at-all, and I remembered that it was Ivan's story about her aunt Cathy, girlfriend of one of her many uncles and no actual legal relation in any way at all, that made me explain during one long car ride about *machatunim*. It's a Yiddish word, sometimes translated as "co-inlaws"—as in, your kid's spouse's parents—it's been used my whole childhood to indicate all those people to whom one is not actually related directly but who are definitely family, like it or not. Your brother's wife's sister. Your former stepmother, no longer married to your dad but still beloved by you, and her new husband. Your favourite cousin's lovers, all three of them. Your sister's wife's brace of great aunties; the child you helped parent for the five years you were lovers with her dad; your uncle's ex-girlfriend from two decades ago— *machatunim*. All of them.

It helps to have a word for it, I find. Especially when someone asks if you're family, and you're not sure if you are or not in their definition of the word, which might be a little more conservative than yours. You say, well, he's *machatunim*. Ivan might be the only person in Whitehorse who could define the word *machatunim*, or even pronounce it, but that's okay. Kind of great, really.

My grandma, Rita, is still alive, the youngest of her five siblings and the last one aboveground. She's in okay health, for ninety-two, all things being equal. But they're not. She doesn't know who I am anymore, or my brother, or my dad or uncle either, and for a woman who did the *New York Times* crossword puzzle every day in blue ballpoint pen, that's worse than dying in some ways. She's not in the happy part where she thinks she's twenty and it's springtime and we're all her suitors, either. She knows she can't remember anything. She hates it.

I didn't call Ivan that day, out of stupid reluctance, but I didn't need to worry—two days later she called me. "Hey, brother," she said in that Yukon accent I love, "what's going on? I been thinking about you all day." Storyteller code for "I have plenty of time to listen to you blubber into the phone, and thanks for asking." I told her the whole story, up to and including the stabbed photos and also how my grandma had been found, outside at six a.m., wandering in her socks three days before, but no one had called us. Ivan hates it, too.

I never met Ivan's little gran, and she's never met my grandma. But I could tell Florence Daws stories, as many of them as Ivan could probably tell Rita Bergman stories, down to the inflection on a "Well, now" or a "That's the problem"; it's how storytellers cement our bond: we start telling each other's family stories. Ivan of the thirty-six first cousins probably doesn't have much to worry about in memorializing Flo; some dozen of them got memorial tattoos that very week, and any number of great- or great-great-grandbabies stand a reasonable chance of having Florence as a middle name, at the very least, if they're not being named for Norse gods (family joke).

But as one of only two keepers of my grandma's stories, I have to say, knowing that somewhere, at any moment, Ivan might, possibly, could be telling the story about the marbled ice cream cake or how she used to steal her father's car from outside the synagogue makes my family stories feel like they're in good hands, in a good mouth, especially as the mouth I have loved most to hear them in falls silent.

(Please imagine here the sound of the storyteller taking a long deep breath, and blowing it out slowly.)

There's one more part to this piece—one more thing I haven't told you. On the day I was writing this, the very day, I talked to Ivan and it turned out that she was almost at the same moment writing a story about her little gran, Florence Daws, and how she missed her. We'd both been noodling around in the subject. Among our noodles, we had both written descriptions of what our grandmothers' heavens would be like, and we read them to one another and had a laugh through our tears.

I feel uncomfortable about mine. Partly because Jews don't really believe in heaven or hell, it's all pretty much The World To Come, and even that doesn't get much airtime in my denominations. Jews are practically and presently concerned with the now and the real—there's no forgiveness from G-d until you've been forgiven by the person you wronged. So writing about heaven seems complicated in that way, plus—and this is the real sticking point—she's not dead yet. Her body's not. She is still, as of today, quite alive.

But this last bit gives you quite a sense of her, and I don't want you just to remember that she was angry and confused and losing her mind. I want you to know her how she was, almost my entire lucky life. So:

In her heaven, there's *Jeopardy!* or professional basketball on TV all the time, with no repeats, and the news programs have news on them and never any weather or "feature stories," and these are interspersed with a show where for a dollar you can throw rotten fruit at George W. Bush. Grandpa is there, for breakfast and dinner each day and to sleep next to at night, each of them whichever age they liked best, but she goes out to lunch by herself with Nancy Ampel and Esther Temlock and has big, meaty sandwiches that don't upset her diabetes or her digestion at all. The solitaire

deck reshuffles itself, and the *NYT* crossword is delivered three
times a day on either the Wednesday, Thursday, or Friday level
of difficulty only, and sweets and good coffee are delivered along
with it, after every meal. She has her teeth back, and her knees
and all her hair, and her slim ankles and she can wear sophisticated clothes every day that fit her perfectly, because she's the
daughter of a tailor and she *hates* clothes that are too big. About
one day every other week she can go in to teach third-graders
whose spelling and manners are great, who want to show her all
their paintings and teach her how to do the new cool dance, which
isn't vulgar at all. World leaders come every evening to be grilled
and scolded, and when they're done its live baroque, jazz, or klez-
mer—depending on her mood—until bedtime. It's always sixty-
five degrees and sunny with a nice breeze outside, and there's lox
and bagels every morning at breakfast, and everyone thinks she's
the smartest one there.

Hiddur Mitzvah

On Fridays, for Shabbos, we bring out the Shabbos things, the items made beautiful by custom and law—*hiddur mitzvah* is the term for this, the enhancing of a good deed by making the objects used in it beautiful as a way to sanctify the act and praise HaShem who commanded it. In our house, as in many houses with multiple generations of Jews and Jewish relatives, the objects are ... well. Hodge-podge would be a kind term.

We have two *challah* covers, one that my husband Ishai was given as a gift upon the occasion of his conversation to Judaism and one that my mother needlepointed for me when she was going through her needlework phase, because no one wanted a new *tallit*. Our Shabbos candlesticks are battered and brass, a set I must have purchased at some stage and have used off-and-on for twenty years, reluctant to buy myself a set when I know that both of my grandmothers, still living, have beautiful ones that I will want to use when the time comes. These, in the meantime, have a somewhat utilitarian nature, but they're familiar and therefore comforting. Our *Kiddush* cup belonged to my Nana Janie, my great-grandmother in my maternal line, and if you've never had the experience of watching your toddler son wrap his chubby little baby paws around the silver cup his great-great-grandmother got as a wedding present and take a baby sip of Shabbos wine, I'll just say: It's pretty great.

We try to always have guests for Shabbos dinner on a Friday

night. We don't always manage to get to *shul* on a Saturday morning, because Saturday mornings are also gay dad's day at the local queer centre on the first Saturday and queer parents' mixer on the fourth Saturday, and this is also part of the deal. We want to make sure, for good and all, that our son Stanley knows plenty of other kids with queer parents and as many other kids with two trans dads as we can manage—not easy, but not impossible. And at the same time, I grew up in a synagogue and all the grownups had known me forever, and my memories of *kiddush* and laughter and making holidays with the same people my entire life are so rich, and so present, and kept me so connected to my congregation—and to my Jewish identity—even when forces of queerness started to seem like they might push me further away. The Sosteks, the Friedlanders, the Weisses, the Fischlers, the Arbeits: they welcomed baby-queer-me with tenderness, and ran interference with my parents about it for, oh, a decade. Ish.

But Friday nights, we get the job done. Dinner, *challah* from Harbord Bakery, which they keep for us now in a paper bag marked Bergman to make sure we always get one. I am not always the one to pick it up, but Ishai, whose last name is Wallace, decided we would get on the list faster with a more recognizably Jewish surname. I light candles and we make scooping motions with our hands and pour the Shabbos light over our son and, if they're into it, our guests. We pour a Kiddush cup of wine and share it, we all touch the bread and make a *motzi*, the blessing over bread, and then Ishai and I feed each other the first morsel, which still feels really, really nice. The candlelight does what candlelight is supposed to do, especially when combined with wine. We're all lovely and peaceful, even when the little dude starts campaigning for ice cream ten seconds after dinner has started.

He gets ice cream on Shabbos, that's what he remembers. After candles and wine, then there's ice cream. So, where is it?

And we invite people to share. Our kitchen table seats six, and we can—with judicious use of stools—expand to eight. We try to make a mix—some people with whom we've shared a lot of Shabbos, and some who are new friends. It takes a certain level of tolerance to come to dinner at our house, since the hosts disappear in turn after dinner to bathe the toddler and put him to bed, and often there is a command performance of story reading in the middle there. Stanley does *not* like to feel left out.

It's the way of having kids that religious observances tend to centre on them for a while when they're little. You can only do as much as the kid will sit through. That's all. So bringing friends and family to share Shabbos dinner is a way to both make sure we get to see them since we now go to bed at ten most nights and make sure that Stanley never remembers not knowing them. To make sure they feel like *family*, like *mishpokhe*, his auntie Abi and his sparkle Chris and his Tante Hanne and uncle Zev and his uncles Nik and Syrus and little cousin Amelie, their brand-new baby daughter. To whom he is not, in any sense, *related*, except that, of course and absolutely, these people are family.

I might have been older than Stanley is now when I first discovered that you could use those kinds of words—words that are heavy with default meanings, words that everyone understands—to make space for relationships that *not* everybody would understand. My son's got a couple of cousins like this, including Morgan, the teenager that I usually shorthand to "my niece," even though the actual explanation has no siblings in it whatsoever. Ishai, my husband, refers to her as "the household teenager," Stanley talks about her as his cousin, and she refers to us as "her other parents," in some situations and "her uncles" in others. I think of them as words that already have so much meaning they won't mind, or maybe notice, if we slip our meaning in there as well. People don't ask her, they just assume, oh, your uncle, brother of your mother or father. No one jumps straight to "Oh, your uncle, husband of your parents' former live-in lover."

Now we have this kid of our own, a kid whose family tree is practically bent double with relatives of assorted kinds—blood, marriage, wine, and glitter—my parents' closest friends, our closest friends, legitimate blood relations, and people who declared upon Stanley's arrival in the world their intention to be his family. The person whose proper title, if we were being literal about this sort of a thing, is "person with whom Papa has had the longest and most tumultuous love affair and working relationship of his life" has claimed for herself the title "Fairy Godsmother." Okay, fair enough. Come for Shabbos, next time you're in town.

(She does.)

I could grade and assign distinctions, to be sure. In town, out of town, related by blood or marriage, wine or glitter, but I don't for two reasons: one, too many people are in more than one category and two, where's the fun in that? Part of what I adore about the family that has coalesced around our Shabbos table and around our son is how magnificently diverse it is, in every way, how many genders and sensibilities and gets of interests and politics and points-of-view it contains, how many tattoos and how many piercings, how many racial and ethnic and religious combinations. I also adore how very befuddled my parents are by the recognition that, if their grandson is related to this mélange of people, then there is some way—however small—in which *they* are related to the lot of them too. Heh.

When Stanley was born, his Tante Hanne—my dear friend and collaborator, who has no children—sent Stanley her childhood baby blanket and her father's old cloth picture books from childhood. They're marvellous—the blanket is made of a pure white wool, spun soft, with the edges hand-bound for a long life. It was made for Hanne upon the occasion of her birth by her own great-grandmother, and passed to Stanley through his nontraditional family ties. His Fairy Godsmother Kate, who has never met her own grandchildren because she is estranged from her only child, carries photos and videos of Stanley on her phone and shows them off as much as I do—okay, well, almost as much. His Grandspuncle and Grandsparkle—the parents of his Spuncle Jacob, obviously—*kvell* over his every milestone with obvious delight and forward the emails and photos of him I send to a truly astonishingly large group of people. They seem to have no concern about explaining that their son, the heteroflexible rabbi, has made a kind of queer family with two transguys via both intention and sperm, and is now known to a rambunctious three-year-old as Spuncle Jacob.

Spuncle, by the way, is the portmanteau word made of "sperm" and "uncle" that our very earnest lesbian friends—one of whom is my husband's oldest friend in the world—made up. They do not appear to notice that the word "spunk" also appears in this word, and it is therefore a little giggleworthy to the gay boys. Their two kids, whom we will become guardian to if, G-d forbid, anything were to happen to them, are some more of Stanley's cousins of no consanguinity whatsoever. It's their son Eli who, in his retelling of the Nativity story, relates that "Mary wanted to have a baby, so she asked her friends for a cup of sperm," because in his world, that's how babies are made. Hard to argue.

The world around Stanley is even more robust than he knows, because he's still little and the people come around one or two or a dozen at a time. He's never been able to play with all his cousins at once. He has no idea how deep he is in *mishpokhe*, how many people claim him as their own.

This is exactly what I want for him. We fly places and Skype with people and do all manner of things to keep him connected and deepen the connections that exist, making Shabbos even when we're exhausted because it's where these things happen. Where the same faces appear over and over, where new friends and new jokes and new stories come to the table, where the old things get pulled out and polished and used with a certain mixture of reverence and work-a-day trust in their abilities, where every object and person and relationship has a story—where it came from, how we met it, what we thought at first, what we understand to be true now.

We tell and retell the stories so he will have heard them a million times before he's old enough to retell them once, and so he understands how much the story of a person or a thing can add to the enjoyment of them, and maybe most so that we can pull them out and polish them as well, tighten them up as storytellers will always and instinctively do with jokes or stories each time they tell them: make them a little better. Make them a little more beautiful with each retelling, fulfilling the obligation of *hiddur mitzvah*: making each story beautiful, in praise to HaShem, who has blessed us a million times with the winding of our stories together.

Engagement

When I was almost thirty, my grandma was in one of her periodic phases of trying to give me everything in the house, anything I wanted. Twenty-eight-year-olds do not understand this impulse, mostly, I think—not twenty-eight-year-olds with the full privilege of good health and the expectation of a long life. Usually I would decline everything she offered, as gently as possible, taking perhaps one small thing to appease her. On this visit, however, her opening salvo in the game hit me right in the heart. That small, burst-open place hasn't healed over even yet, not that I'd want it to.

(Sometimes I think that's the defining characteristic of a story-teller. These wounds, we kind of treasure them, because they keep us open to things. Anyhow.)

In her octogenarian hand, she held a tiny ring. Smaller than I could wear even on my pinky finger, dull gunmetal grey. Even still, she handled it like it was the richest treasure. She told me it had been a gift from my Grandpa while he was away at war; he had torn a piece of steel off the wing of a downed German Messerschmitt and taken it to a jeweller when he had some leave to be melted down and formed into a ring. When he got it back, he engraved it (using some improvised wartime method) with a Star of David and the words *Adonai Shaddai* in Hebrew—G-d Almighty. Then he sent his love token, wrested out of a Nazi warplane and turned into a celebration of a Jew in love, to his fiancée in Massachusetts.

Tears came to my eyes as I held it. I asked my grandma if it was all right with Grandpa that she give it to me and she asked in reply, who else on earth would get it, now or ever? Better I should take it, she said. Grandpa stroked his softened finger across the face of it once and agreed. It was for me.

For years, I didn't know what to do with it. I experimented with wearing it on a chain which was uncomfortable; I looked into having it made bigger and was told it might get ruined if I tried. I was married at the time, to a woman it might have fit, but I somehow didn't want to give it to her. It felt almost unbearable, to have perhaps the only piece of handed-down jewellery I would ever really, really want to wear from one of my female relatives and not be able to wear it.

I visited it often. It rested in the jewellery chest that holds my collection of cufflinks and tie tacks and watches, small and spare among the shiny things. I used to talk to it, completely unself-conscious at the time, encouraging it to be proud of itself. That it was worth more to me than all the other items in the box put together. Than all the other objects I owned, put together. But even still, I couldn't wear it.

Intermittently, someone would suggest I have it made into a pin, a pendant, a tie-bar. I would have worn it in my nose before I would have had it altered, but none of those were options. And yet there it sat, in the green-felt lined drawer of the box, by itself.

Eventually I met the person to whom I wanted to present it. It wasn't long after meeting Ishai that I knew I wanted to marry him, just as—evidently—it wasn't long after meeting my grandma that my grandpa knew he wanted to marry her. After he died and my Grandma lost her mind, we went through her things and discovered that at some point during the same war he had paid to have his photo taken at a studio in Paris, just so he could send it to my grandma. At the top, his inscription read:

To Mrs Bergman—

(Hey! I like the sound of that!)

with love from your Stan

It occurs to me, as time has passed and I get to know this grand-father through the lens of what he left behind in objects and actions, that I get my incurable romantic streak from him. I know for sure that he's the only member of my family besides me known to have performed multiple acts of ridiculous international gift-giv-ing. When Ishai and I first met, and had the magical night that led to the incredible weekend that let to the summer that led to our wedding, I missed him so much after our weekend together that I FedExed my socks to Canada. To him.

Not just my socks, though, oh no. Also an iPod shuffle, a little silver one, because I had started out trying to make him a mix-CD and discovered I had too much music I wanted to send, and then thought about sending two CDs, labelled Side A and Side B, and then I outgrew those and considered a Vol. I, Vol. II, Vol. III scheme until the ridiculousness of it all broke over me like a wave and I just said fuck it and filled up the shuffle. I put in my own copies of two of my favourite books, *Ex Libris* by Anne Fadiman (a book of essays about books) and *A Blind Man Can See How Much I Love You* by Amy Bloom, with their curling covers and broken spines. I added a couple of high-end chocolate bars, and then—then I was overwhelmed with wanting to send some-thing of me. I might have sent a T-shirt or a hoodie, some item of my giant clothing like I'd given to all manner of close people across my life. But in this case, I knew he was embroiled in hard things with his not-quite-ex, with whom he was still living and so, ludicrously, I added to the package a pair of my socks. White, with navy heels and toes, plain and handsome, just enough of a thing that he could wear them and think of me without drawing the attention (or ire) of the not-quite-ex. This is still referred to as the time I FedExed my socks to Canada—and remains one of my better decisions.

The desire to reach out remains strong; the hunger of sending a piece of where I am to the place I'm not feels the same to me as I think it must have to my grandfather, though I am never in as much danger as he was and never for so long either. But if you peeked into the files of any of the people to whom I write regular paper letters while on the road, you'd find a hilarious assortment of items—menus and handbills and posters and notices, used as stationery and sent away out of the urgent, insistent need to have something of where I am in common with them wherever they are, even if only in the future. The ring my grandfather made for my grandmother on the battlefields of World War II is certainly a better heirloom, more interesting and more beautiful, than the notice from the Government of Canada about the phasing out of the penny on which I recently wrote a letter to my beloved friend Hanne. But it springs from the same want, the same desire to fold the wibbly-wobbly timey-wimey stuff until the ends touch. Even a little, just for a moment.

Ishai wears the ring my grandpa made and sent to my grandma, now, and I love to see it on his hand even though sometimes I have to take very deep breaths when I think about him losing it. Typically, I am of the "it's only a thing" school about objects. At university, I read a *Reader's Digest* article in a waiting room some-where about a father who had slipped a note into his daughter's glove box, alongside the auto insurance paperwork and registra-tion folder. The note read: "In case of accident, remember: it's you

I love, not the car." I found this so satisfying that I immediately did the same thing in the glove box of my own car, in case one of the many friends who borrowed it had an accident. Things, even nice things, can be repaired or replaced. I know as I type it that this comes only partly from my non-attachment and the other part from my class privilege, but even still, it's how I am. Things are things. Another thing can be got, found, made, bartered, or bargained for.

But not this ring. If given the opportunity to save a single object from a consuming fire, I would choose it. If it were lost, I honestly cannot say for sure that I would ever stop missing it. Five years later I still miss my grandfather, long after grief is evidently supposed to have smoothed out its jagged places, so sharp today that I burst into tears in the bathtub when I realized how much I wanted to talk to him about the thing that was vexing me. I tried the tactic where you address the dead jocularly and try to answer yourself in their voice and cried harder. I am crying as I type, breathing through what's hard so I can imagine what's good— where is he now? Wherever it is, I imagine that he is sending me things from there, things that compress the vast gap between us down to nothing just for an instant, in order for us to touch. However briefly.

Having come to this thought, I am now clear about what the thing is—what the gift is that my grandfather, Stanley Bergman, would have made out of whatever he has to hand and sent me so I can be with him even in sadness. I pick it up from preschool in the evenings and bring it home and feed it the pierogi I got today at the market because some little gifts like pierogi. He'll demand to snuggle before I'm finished eating; he'll want to play the new game I just taught him and then he'll want another chapter from the *Just So Stories*. Probably today I will be more patient with his various hijinks and nonsense than I sometimes am, fresh in this understanding. I've known all along that he was a gift, and in some ways he's the gift of a lot of people to me. In the fullness of time, maybe also a gift from us to other people.

But there's this thing my Stanley does, this smile. It's not a smirk, but it's mischievous and full of a lark. It's a catch-me-if-you-can kind of a smile. Let me be clear—there's not a drop of my blood in that kid's veins; we're genetic strangers to each other. So there's no skip-a-generation descendency to explain it. But that smile—I knew it already before I ever saw him smile it, even if I didn't understand until I started telling this particular story whose smile it was. I couldn't quite see, until I started writing, what gift I was getting and from whom.

Thanks, Grandpa. I miss you too.

Sharon, Who Never Visits

I haven't seen my grandma in a year as of this writing. That's far longer than I have ever gone in my entire life, and I am constantly aware of it. I have not seen the room in which she currently lives, nor the new bed in which she sleeps. I haven't seen which art she kept, which photos she kept, which small things travelled with her when she moved; I don't know what she looks like right now or which size of her clothes she's wearing or how her face has changed.

The last time I saw my grandma was Passover, last year. She was already in the deeper phases of dementia, already starting to forget the words for things and the relationships between people, already a little unclear in moments about who was who. But even still, she was clear enough to look at me and say, "I think I know you but I'm not sure. Who are you?"

"I used to be Sharon," I said, "but now I'm called Sason. I'm Sason Bear Bergman. I'm your granddaughter."

"And him?" she asked, gesturing to my son Stanley. "Is he yours? How did you get him?"

"He's mine, yes. My son. Our son."

She looked at me a long time, mouth opening and closing again. My family members all jumped in and offered various other explanations; I remember it like an explosion of talking somewhere behind my head. They were all trying to help, I know perfectly well; all trying to create a narrative that best matched what they thought my grandmother would be able to comprehend. I sat quietly, looking at her calmly and steadily; I could tell that she was trying to put together the pieces of who I was, who she remembered me to be, why I was there. My heart broke to watch it but I stayed present, hoping that my plain being with it might help her to feel what she'd felt when we would sit together, and make the connection.

She shook her head and waved her hands, dismissing the problem as too complicated. A silence fell, and we changed the subject. But all day she kept looking at me, trying to sort me out. Trying to understand.

That morning, she'd known me. That very morning there had been a scare—she was staying at a nearby hotel with an accessible room, and my father had hired an aide to arrive each morning, help her get up and bathed and dressed and breakfasted, and accompany her down to the lobby so we could pick her up for the day. The same aide arrived back in the evening for the reverse duty, helping my grandmother out of her clothes and into her nightgown, handling her dentures and so forth. But in this morning, my grandma wasn't in the lobby. She didn't answer her room phone. I almost contained my panic, went and got a manager who let me into the room, and found my grandma stuck on the toilet, unable to get herself off. No way to know how long she'd been there. She was angry and humiliated and grateful to see me—she recognized me then, and was calm and comfortable in my presence as I helped her off the toilet and back to the bed. I got her undressed and dressed again and discovered that putting clothes on a ninety-two-year old is more or less exactly like putting clothes on a two-year-old except for the bra. I felt competent; I went slowly and kept my hands gentle and kind on her skin as I moved her, just as I do for my small son, but with a lump in my throat and the prickle of tears in my eyes. I did not want her to need this kind of tending, even though I was glad to be able to offer it.

(We will not discuss what I, and then my father, said to the owner of the service whose employee simply fucked off and left my grandmother stranded on her toilet in an unfamiliar hotel room for more than an hour as far as I can tell. The sentiments expressed were not kind.)

In the moment before I collected her up off the toilet, lightweight in my arms, I prayed a quick and fervent prayer that she would recognize me, that I could be her granddaughter right then. It worked, and the rescue proceeded without interruption, but by evening she clearly didn't remember. I think we must have used up the last of the recognition, right then in the crisis, and afterward ... no more. She looked at me and shook her head, like you might at having spotted your college roommate's ex-boyfriend across a cocktail party—yes, he looks familiar, but you're pretty sure you're not really expected to remember him.

It's understandable. I both had and hadn't changed—except for sprouting a goatee and cutting my hair into a flattop, I didn't look so different from ten years before. But the connection between this guy standing in front of her and the granddaughter she remembered wouldn't spark. There was no conductive fluid in which they could meet; the thing dry-fired a few times and sputtered to a stop. I wasn't anyone, anymore.

I took a few months off from visiting, and then went again when I felt too distant from her. I went cautiously; it was one of the last visits she received in her own apartment. Just a few days later, they moved her to one room with its own bathroom, no oven or stovetop, more monitoring. When I arrived with my small son, she was clearly delighted by him, but equally clearly convinced that I was my brother. She addressed me by his name; I tried to correct her a few times and then just started answering to it. We watched Stanley caper about and climb on things and be gorgeous and charming and full of little songs and she smiled. She laughed. We went back the next day for more of the same: more smiling and laughing, more baby hugs and kisses, more of the understanding that I was my younger brother. At that point, he and his just-then-one-year-old twins hadn't yet packed up their entourage and made the journey, so she hadn't seen the boys except briefly, at their *brit milot*. In her head, I think, she had conflated us with him and his kids. People kept talking about her new great-grandsons and that made sense, why, here was a new great-grandson right here! Wonderful.

I left feeling pretty good about the weekend. I wanted her to feel loved—and enviable, too, so I contrived for one of the short visits to be right in the lobby where all the passersby could see her being climbed all over by her gorgeous little great-grand-baby. That all succeeded, and I got to see my uncles too and spend some time with other local friends, and everything was great until two weeks later. I called her, and her aide answered, and when I said who it was she said, "Oh, Miss Bergman just asked about you, Sharon. She was asking, when do you ever come to visit?"

Suddenly, like someone had dumped a bucket of ice water over my head, I understood. She had no idea I'd just been there. She thought it was Jeffrey. She thought she had a grandson who visited her, often, diligently, and then that other worthless one, Sharon, who never bothered to visit. I felt like I'd been gut-kicked by a mule. I got off the phone, and I cried until I puked from the wave of loss pulling me under and holding me there.

I was prepared to lose some things when I started living mostly as a man in the world. I said goodbye to certain butches and certain femmes, to the good queer nod, to women's space, to clean public bathrooms, to admiring the babies of strangers, to a full head of hair, to being assumed to be safe, to recognition as that honestly magnificent creature, the butch. I didn't want to lose them, but I traded them for other things and, whatever the costs, I knew they were worth what I got in return. But not this. Not this moment like an icicle replacing my spine, with my grandma—my grandma who had been my ally and confidant since I was born—now spending the end of her days miserably imagining that I (who had been her ally and confidant too) had just given up on her when things had gotten bad and hard. She remembered that I existed. She just thought I didn't care anymore.

There's no ending to this piece. I wasn't able to bring myself to go back for a year. Part of me was afraid I would just confuse her, part of me just couldn't bear the thought of the possibility that she might ask—where was Sharon? What would I say? I'm her? I used to be her? She's gone now? All the possibilities were equally horrifying, and then just when I resolved that I was going to go anyway, she had a bad phase of anger and paranoia and I was discouraged from going at all for a while.

I'm going again, in a month. I'll say I'm whoever I think she might recognize; I don't care. She doesn't really know anyone anymore, but she likes visitors and pictures of the children. I will try not to cry on her. I will try to keep from upsetting her. I will try to be a pleasure and a comfort. But I'll wait until she dozes off, as she does a lot now, and then I'll sit by her bedside when her eyes are closed and tell her, over and over again, who I am, and that I love her. That Sharon does visit. She does. It's hard to see, grandma, but I swear to G-d she does.

Let Them Be a Symbol Before Your Eyes

I have all sorts of marks on my body from a lifetime of engaging in various pursuits. A mild dimple on my forehead from getting smacked in the head by a baseball bat while playing softball when I was nine, a huge gash on my shin from stepping into an uncovered pool skimmer while lifeguarding at seventeen, a scar that looks rather like a map of the Hawaiian Islands just above one knee that I have no memory of getting whatsoever, plus the usual array of odd spots, silvery lines, nicks and divots you get when you're not too careful but typically pretty game. I also have either four tattoos or five, depending on how you count it, and one thin raised line of a scar straight down the line of my breastbone from a cutting meant to be both decorative and symbolic.

I like body modifications, generally—I find many of them beautiful and even when I don't care for them aesthetically; I have some deep fondness for the choice to make a mark upon oneself as a way of signifying something. Sometimes it's a fairly complex thing we are signifying and sometimes a relatively mundane thing, but whether you have Tigger kicking a soccer ball tattooed on your butt or the name and favourite flower of your deceased beloved inked over your heart, I appreciate it. I have my feelings about having assorted concepts written in other alphabets and similar tattooing behaviours, but that's another day's essay.

This one is about what happens to those marks when whatever prompted us into them fades or leaves or becomes difficult. What happens when we change our allegiances or our circumstances?

I have four or possibly five tattoos (I have my son's footprints on my thighs, right where he used to love to stand on my lap as a baby. One footprint per thigh could be counted as two separate tattoos, but I think of it as one tattoo). One is a piece I got for my now-ex-wife. I intended it as an act of love and also binding, an image of the southern hemisphere constellation Apus, the bird. I had always called her *little bird*, and for a while I looked for bird images to get but didn't find anything I wanted—not a screaming eagle, not a hipster swallow, not a fat little singin' cartoon bird ... none of them seemed right. We had a motif of stars in our love talk after I once very nerdily quoted a poem about them to her, and suddenly one day while looking at a star map, I had a brainwave. A constellation in the shape of a bird. Yes.

I got the Apus tattoo, placed at the exact spot on my thigh where she used to rest her hand when I drove, as a way of letting that experience of being loved show in my body in a legible, visible way. It's worth noting that I have exceptionally sensitive skin and am kind of a big wuss about pain besides, so getting a tattoo is never an easy process. I stick it out because I want the art, not because I enjoy the experience (as some people do). But tattoos are wounds—thousands of tiny holes poked in the skin to bring the ink in—and the thing about an opening is that it's designed to let things move through. Out and also in. A tattoo felt like a way to draw some of the love I felt for her into my body and then mark the spot of it with a decoration. I suffered gladly and walked home from the tattoo studio slowly.

Now, ten years later, I'm no longer married to Nicole, and I have some rather complicated feelings about the tattoo. Likewise, the decorative cutting I have that was made by my former lover Skian in a particularly tender moment, and for a very similar value of opening and letting love in, has stayed visible on my skin for most of the last decade. When he made the mark, I did quite a bit to make sure it would scar, and it worked—I can see the line clearly. Every day. All the time. He and I haven't spoken in some years now, and I similarly have any number of feelings about my cutting, none of them straightforward.

In Judaism—which people say disapproves of tattooing but which actually disapproves of "mutilation," not typically understood to be the same thing—we are reminded in the *V'ahavta* to make our commitments to HaShem known and visible. Bind them as a sign upon your hand, the prayer says, and let them be a symbol before your eyes; set them on the doorposts of your house and upon your gates. There's a value in declaring yourself, a virtue in it. This propensity has gotten us in trouble over and over again across the ragged plain of history; we've been rounded up and killed or exiled any number of times for being Jews and it's relatively easy to do because all of our houses have *mezuzot* on them. But it also shows you what door to knock on if you're a Jew in trouble.

Mezuzot, however, can be taken down if need be—if you move house or to repaint or whatever. Marks to the skin are permanent, and though they can sometimes be covered or given laser treatment to shrink or lighten them, they never completely go away. Even if it's what we dearly want, we always know what *was* there.

Ultimately, I have decided not to remove or change the marks I have, even when they're from love that's soured or they call to people who are completely beyond my reach now for whatever reason. Instead, my choice is to let them stand as the moment they were. I got both the tattoo and the cutting because I wanted them. I got them in love, I got them with excitement; I touched them with the very tips of my fingers for weeks and months afterward in hard moments so I could feel their slightly raised contours on my skin. I showed them off. I cared for them diligently, so I wouldn't ruin my marks, and I knew when I was getting them that they'd last as long as this physical body holds out. They're mine.

I got them in good faith and with a full heart, which is ultimately more than I can say for most of the marks and scars on my body, even though I accept them without upset. The pool skimmer injury took the flesh off my shin right to the bone and made me cry, as did the bat to the head (though I was nine at the time and my crying was a little more forgivable). There's a light seam under my lower lip from a car accident in which I not only got badly hurt but wrecked a great old car, and I see that in the mirror every day, too. It doesn't trouble me especially to still have it, even though the day on which I got it was awful, really awful. So it seems to me that if I can live with the mementoes of terrible days on my skin, then I can also live with the memories of really great days.

Sometimes, true, this is easier said than done. The physical injuries have healed over and never pain me anymore, but the injuries to my tender heart still twinge in certain kinds of emotional weather. It's very difficult to have someone who was your family for a long time turn themselves away from you, and that kind of wound is far less precise, far less controlled than the ones I had inflicted for love and beauty. It's a ragged mess, is what it is, and it runs so deep that it has to heal by what medical professionals call "primary intention." That's what it's called when the injury exists through so many bodily layers that it cannot be sutured lest the skin and facia heal before the underlying tissues do, causing infection or "failure to heal" without the light and air circulation required. When healing by primary intention—either from a physical wound or an emotional one—there's very little to do but keep the site clean, stay well-hydrated, and wait while your body or mind marshals its resources and knits you back together fibre by fibre. It takes a while and no one has any fun, but it's the best way to heal completely.

I look at the marks of my past family every day, the visible ones, the ones that live on my skin. They've long since healed over; they no longer open me to anything. But they're a part of me, of my experience, as much a record of what has come before as any of the others and in some ways more so since I took them on purposefully. They're choices I made. Even if it is true that we're counselled to pack away our love letters and our old photos of our lost loves if we want to truly heal from breakups or divorce, my wearing the tokens I couldn't just pack away ensured that I have struggled and mourned until I healed. That's worth something. It's also worth something to remember that even if things ended (and not even all that well), I loved and was loved, risked and was safely caught. In the end, I don't want to cover that or erase it—I want to celebrate it and carry it forward. The tattoo of Stanley's left foot on my right thigh is a centimetre at most from the constellation on the same thigh. Like an old tree, I wear every year that I've lived inside me, drought or flood, long winter or warm fall, all of them legible in my rings and— like on any old tree—once they become part of the whole, they're beautiful.

Get Up Everybody and Sing

I remember feeding him ice-cold watermelon I ran into a bodega for. I remember how hot it was that day, the day of Stonewall 25, how so many more of us turned up to march than they expected and we clogged the streets. The youth contingent was toward the end so we could get the biggest cheers when we entered because youth contingents were a lot smaller in 1994 than they are today, but anyhow—it was broiling hot, almost 100 in the sun and there wasn't any shade, so I took the extra twenty dollars I had stolen from my mother's wallet that morning and went into a bodega looking for something we could use to take the edge off. It was cool inside, and dim, and in the back a much older woman was cutting a watermelon into cubes and putting the cubes into clamshells. "2 FOR $5," the sign said, and I asked very politely if I could have one of the large, salad bar containers of watermelon for five dollars instead. She agreed, also very politely. I forced myself back out into the hot mid-day street with my treasure in my hands, back to the knot of kids I had been getting to know all morning, back when we were kids and not "youth" and no one complained about ageism because us kids could just yell louder and so we did. That morning, we were chanting and cheering, "Two-four-six-eight! How do you know your kids are straight? One-three-five-nine! Queer kids are mighty fine!" and "I love you, you love me, ho-mo-sex-u-ality, people think, we're just friends, but we're really *lesbians!*" I loved you immediately because you screamed loudest when proclaiming yourself a lesbian, even though you were at that moment a handsome chunky fella and not lesbian-looking at all. I was there with my college girlfriend, who was never very nice to me, but when I emerged blinking into the brutal sunshine it wasn't her fever I was thinking about cooling with the cold, sweet fruit. I had a different fruit in mind, and when I got back to the group and popped the lid she complained that I hadn't brought forks, but you opened wide and I came close and put my treasure right on your tongue. You sighed and chewed and licked your lips and wriggled a little against me, the sweat of your sun-warmed chest and belly shining on my leather suspenders when you pulled away, and then you opened your mouth back up and said, "More, please." I fed you again, holding the container of watermelon up and away with one hand so other people would know they could also help themselves while I attended to your hungers, and you made a joke about how you black boys loved your watermelon. I didn't know if I should or could laugh at the joke when a black boy said it himself, and it threw me out of the moment. Finally I said, "I usually yell at people for saying things like that," and you said, in the most flirtatious tone you could imagine, "Oh, am I in trouble? Will there be punishment?" and there I was, back on solid ground again. I stuffed his mouth with watermelon until the juice overflowed and he smiled and swallowed and smiled and swallowed with the whole queer world swirling around us in the bright sun until my girlfriend pulled me away because the march was finally, after hours upon hours, starting to move. I could tell you today from memory the exact angle of his slightly crooked front tooth or the pattern of tiny whorls in his chest hair, more like dots than anything, but I don't know his name and I never knew it, which I don't mourn. We were there together for that moment, hot and close and fruit sugar on our lips, being queer in the sun like we came to be. I would have gladly enjoyed more but I didn't need it; we knew how to draw each other in.

I remember that I was sixteen when I saw the AIDS quilt, not all of it but a large portion, displayed at Harvard, and I wasn't ready for it, not nearly; I don't think anyone ever is. I also remember only one panel—a huge white square with a Star of David embroidered in the middle, a shimmering watery blue of metallic thread, and beneath it, in silver letters, the Hebrew word *Zachor*. Remember. I dissolved. I started to cry—again—and reflexively I started to say Kaddish, the Jewish prayer for the dead while standing in a gymnasium with the faint smell of smart-kid sweat socks still lingering in the air, echoing and lonely in the way that only a gym can be echoing and lonely especially for a picked-last kid like me, choking out the words of Kaddish between ugly, ugly crying, hitching and gasping, with the snot running down my face unchecked and soaking my shirt collar. I was barely through the first line before a hand slipped into mine and a voice joined me, a gaunt and grizzled fag whose own Kaddish probably didn't wait a year, and then a hand on my shoulder, and then the heat of another human behind me, all leaning their heads close into mine and grieving with me for these dead who were neither friends nor strangers, but still family. By the time I had finished the prayer, taken deep breaths and tried to calm down and failed and cried some more, there were a dozen people huddled around me, red-eyed and lovely, speaking the same cadence of Hebrew in a prayer for the dead. When the first of my fellow mourners started to crumple, I caught him and held him close, cheek to cheek like this was the school gymnasium of the grade-eight dance and we were the awkward grade-eight slow-dancers of forever, his spit and snot bubbling as he cried and the bubbles popping into my face. He gasped when he opened his eyes and saw the bubbles, he wailed, "I have AIDS," and I shifted him closer in my arms and murmured into his ear, "It's okay, baby. I promise not to come in your mouth," and as suddenly as he'd started to cry he started to laugh, clapping both his wet hands onto my wet cheeks, holding my face hard and smiling right into my eyes like my backward half-joke was the best gift he could have imagined.

I remember standing in the hallway outside that cancelled panel with the two of them, who I knew a little bit in the way you know someone when you see them at the same conference every year for ten years—and neither of them knew one another at all—in the swirl and midst of a huge international queer movement gathering. I remember falling completely by accident, just because we were all standing there, into an hour's deep talk about words, words and how we use them to hurt and heal and explain during which he, the sign language interpreter, demonstrated the feyest sign I had ever seen for Queer while she and I practiced until he deemed us acceptable, touching our ring fingers to our tongues and flipping our wrists back over our hairstyles over and over. This prompted her to offer us both some glitter, out of the clever small vial of it she had in her bag, and—as when anointed with any holy substance—he and I both bent our heads solemnly so she could sprinkle us generously, our giggles the prayer to sanctify the moment. When we stood up, we both shook our heads slightly to admire the fine shimmer that came down around our shoulders like a mantle and we grinned at each other. I don't know if I stood up a little straighter, but he did for sure while she did her own hair again and we admired her, her verve and her style and the fine, frolicsome way she wore her clothes and her glitter, bright in plumage against a backdrop of people in serious workaday clothes, queering every room she entered. We talked and laughed and groomed each other like monkeys, which they do when they are trying to build trust—whether caring for their babies or trying to coax another monkey up into the tree line for a little monkey-panky—we knew what it was even still and we relaxed into it like the monkeys we are. He showed us how all his D/deaf friends use their smartphones to take photos of the people they meet since names and name-signs don't always make an intuitive match and we put our contacts in each other's phones and took pouting, kissy-face, queer-ass self-portraits in commemoration of our Glitter Hour, glitter that would have felt way too femme for twenty years of my life but which I could accept and even revel in, suddenly, finally, in the hallway with these strangers, who now weren't anymore; I have the pictures to prove it.

I remember all of these times, all of these moments—who knows how many?—all the times I have walked in to a room and felt at home among my family even if I was alone in a strange city, knowing with the certainty of long experience that if I let myself be there I would be drawn in, that my glitter would show, that the Sylvester floating in the fluid of my joints would be audible to the right people. I've known I could be close if I were willing to be close with people without observing the default-world bubble of separateness, a thing I never noticed until the day I stood with all my relatives in the packed lobby of Alice Tully Hall in New York City, us and 700 gay men there to welcome the premiere of the *AIDS Quilt Songbook*—my uncle's poem had been set to music by Ned Rorem, and we were there to applaud his accomplishment. By then I had moved my body in many kinds of queer space so I had no trouble moving through the lobby, a hand on one shoulder or another hip, murmuring and sliding, insinuating myself into gaps without even breaking conversations, our clothes more than enough barrier between us—and then yet another handsome man in yet another tuxedo tried to move past my father that way, and he shattered the buzz of the room, whirling around and biting off a curse mid-word while the man who had simply been trying to get past looked bewildered and affronted. I wasn't afraid or alienated there in the crush, not there or anywhere the queers are—sometimes, yes, where upscale, respectable gay-men-and-lesbians have been, but never in the queer spaces, the odds and ends of the world that no authority cares about so we can fill them with our good art and words and sweat and love and make them a home. I remember the rec rooms and the block parties, the dance clubs and the bookstores, breathing your breaths and feeling your knees against mine, your back against my chest, your head tipped back against me, your wordless smile, the trust of your weight, the sweetness of your open mouth, Sister Sledge ringing our spines, singing at the top of our voices even if we never sing any other song, hips bumping together and hands raised, presenting the truth of our hearts to the world.

Shake the Queer Tree

I got in a lot of trouble once—an irascibly angry, scolding email and a concurrent attempt at trash-talking me all over "town," where town equals friends in common. My crime was sending a last-minute email to an old friend we'll call Louise (not her real name) asking if she could provide an emergency crash space to another old friend with a job interview situation about to be fouled by weather. I copied Louise's roommate Helga (not *her* real name, either), a person I knew slightly, on the email and clicked send. Done. Off to other questions.

I often send these sorts of emails. *Yenta*-mail is what I've always called them, where I send the same email to two people I know and introduce them to one another for the betterment of all. Phil, friend who is moving to Nebraska, meet Pradeep, friend who already lives there. Yonatan, friend who has tenure at University of Fictional Place, meet Lurleen, friend who is considering an offer of employment at/admission to that university. And so on. It's rare for a week to pass in which I don't send some sort of connecting email, either of my own accord or at the request of a friend. If you have ever gotten on social media and asked who knew of a safe place to pitch your tent in Cape Breton, who knew a person of colour who'd been to Space Camp, or who had any recommendation for a vegetarian restaurant in Nachitoches, I probably knew someone.

Honestly, I enjoy this particular kind of work, and I am also happy to respond to the requests and *yenta*-mails of friends. I more or less assume that this is part of the deal—it's what enriches us. The great and sprawling worldwide queer network doesn't always have a lot of cash, but we have tended to be pretty good about being willing to share what we have with friends, or friends of friends, who might need it. Even if letters of introduction have largely fallen out of style now that so many people just use a credit card and the Internet to locate the lodgings and activities of their choice, queers and transpeeps are still using them as a way of identifying safe, welcoming places to stay, or to be.

(Some readers will remember the magazine called *Lesbian Connection* [mailed stapled closed in a plain wrapper] that carried the news and information of the day to lesbians from coast to coast, and included Contact Dykes for various regions. Contact Dykes were volunteers who had published their details so that travellers or people who might be moving could be in touch as they went. I discovered this in the bathroom magazine basket of a long-ago playmate who had once dreamed of a *Lesbian Connection* cross-country road trip and film, and I remain charmed by the idea. I understand that the subscribers are often virulently anti-trans lesbian separatists, but I still admire what they were trying to do there.)

So as a travelling circus and a friendly sort of a fella, I tend to assume that I'm in a better-than-many place to be able to riffle my mental Rolodex and come up with the right person in the right place. On the night in question, with Snowmageddon threatening the Washington, DC, area, I squinted hard and came up with a possibility. I didn't think it was a perfect solution, but it put the one friend within striking distance of the next morning's job interview and so—I thought—why not? Therein lay my egregious crime.

First I got an email from Louise, a queer queerio from way back—so long ago she had a Lesbian Avenger Action Name—to say that she was sorry but logistics made it impossible. My other friend, the travelling one, responded very kindly that she was grateful for their thoughtfulness but might have a solution. Oh, well, I thought. Doesn't always work out. And then, the next day: nastygram from the other roommate.

I didn't understand what this was about, at first. What did she mean I'd been presumptuous and rude? I was outraged by the suggestion. I sputtered and fumed, while simultaneously worrying that my old friend also found me presumptuous and rude. Did everyone, in fact, find all my (ostensibly) helpful *yenta*-ing and connecting to be presumptuous and rude? Suddenly I felt like I'd fallen into the Phillip Lopate poem *"We Who Are Your Closest Friends,"* which begins:

> We who are
> your closest friends
> feel the time
> has come to tell you
> that every Thursday
> we have been meeting
> as a group
> to devise ways
> to keep you
> in perpetual uncertainty
> frustration
> discontent and
> torture

I reacted as well as I ever do to these sorts of personal issues, which is to say, very poorly. First, major crisis of confidence. Then triangulation: call some of the aforementioned old friend's closest people (including her husband, to whom I introduced her) and ask them in faux-casual tones if they know what's going on. Meanwhile, stew over the unpleasant, accusatory email some more while imagining that some new and tragic flaw in my character has been revealed to me. I had been labouring under the impression that I already knew all of my really big faults. Shows what I know.

When I finally spoke with the friend to whom I had tried to send a last-minute houseguest, she was quick and kind to reassure me that no, I hadn't really done anything awful and yes, in fact, she also thought it was just fine. Then she said, in a somewhat confiding tone, "But Helga's ... straight, you know."

I sat with that for a moment, trying to let the understanding sink in. It didn't want to go. It's not that I'm an idiot, you understand—rather, two things were at work. One, I didn't want it to be true that Helga might have a legitimate complaint and not just be a complete gaping asshole. Two, and probably the bigger piece, was being brought face-to-face with how alone I was in my thinking about people caring for each other, even when they might not know one another well. Up until this blistering email, I kind of figured most people would be—at the very least—easy with the idea of taking in a stranger on the recommendation of a friend. Even at the last minute, even if it's not someone they imagine they might otherwise like, they'd still accept it even if they do not, as I tend to, generate a lot of it. Not everyone knows a zillion people and keeps a running mental tally of where they all are and what they all like and need (because, evidently, not everyone is

an adult child of a complex family with many conflicting impera-
tives about "usefulness" and a recovering stage-manager and a
gold-medal Virgo to boot).

Also, admittedly, not everyone is an interdependence junkie, as I
am. That's perfectly fair, I guess, though really not to my personal
taste—I do believe, fervently and deeply, that if we all devoted a
certain amount of our time, energy, and money toward looking
out for others the world would be vastly improved. I try to walk
my talk in this way, at least until I come smack-bang up against
the question of how far to extend the reach of it? The answer to
which question, in my sense of things is: as far as possible. Partly
because that's my general sensibility, but also partly because it
has extended itself so very far for me.

On the trip I took to research my Holocaust show *Monday Night
in Westerbork*, I took advantage of a remarkably cheap plane ticket
that routed me though Manchester airport in England. Taking
no-frills short-hop European airlines like EasyJet and Ryanair from
there saved me hundreds of dollars I didn't have—except that my
return flight left so early in the morning that I would have had to
spend two-thirds of the savings on a crap hotel near the airport
in order to make it work. At the time, it was the choice between
being able to eat three meals a day on the trip or having to make it
work with just a hostel breakfast and one other meal. So, I reached
out—I did what I refer to as shaking the queer tree, and posted a
general plea on my blog for some help with this. Someone I knew
a bit, but with whom I had closer friends in common, contacted
her friends who lived in Manchester and enquired as to whether
they would be willing to take an itinerant writer on for the night,
sight unseen. They wrote back quite promptly and said they'd be
glad to do it. I stayed there for the last night of my very difficult

trip; they sent me painstakingly detailed instructions for the train, met me at the station, fed me a very nice dinner, and we drank wine and talked and got to know each other until rather too late. In the morning, I crept out in the still-dark to go to the airport, leaving behind a wet towel, a gift of Polish plum candies with jam centres, and a thank-you note.

I have dozens of stories like this. I also have hundreds of stories of getting The Family Discount, being offered extra services or a percentage discount just for being queer, out and visibly queer, like the salesclerk at Men's Wearhouse who applied every discount known to her and then an extra "customer service adjustment" equalling a further hundred dollars so I could get both the suits I was holding—one for me, and one for Ishai. We'd gone in because I needed a suit, and when I spotted one that I thought he would look great in, I cajoled him into trying it on. He looked great, indeed, but it was a little more than made sense for us to spend at that moment and he had a former suit of mine to wear, so his need wasn't acute. But she saw us, I think, being sweet to one another; saw the smile crest and break across my face when he emerged from the dressing room looking terrifically handsome. So when I got to the cash with just the one suit, she asked why and then set about fixing the problem. At the very end of the transaction, just as she was handing me the suit bags, she casually said it: "My wife and I ..." Just so I would understand that it was the Family Discount, and not some other machination of commerce or kindness.

(Ishai, who is a magnificent flirt, gets this sort of treatment even more frequently than I do. I once met him off a plane from Chicago to San Francisco to see him disembark carrying a full bottle of nice wine—his gift, along with a first-class seat and extra dessert—from the gentleman flight attendant who'd been on his plane. Well, then.)

People have even, very kindly and generously, been my proxies in this process with no thought of personal gain. When my long-time friend Sean who had just moved to Portland weeks before fell ill with some sort of death flu, he didn't know anyone in town well enough to ask them to go to the grocery store for him. I turned to Facebook. Sarah, a stranger who worked at Powell's Bookstore and had read one of my books, answered my call for help and did for Sean what I wanted to do, but couldn't. She drove to the store and then all the way across town to his house, stocked him up with soup and juice and ginger ale, garlic and lemons and honey and *People* magazine, and let me send her a cheque for what it cost (money I knew Sean didn't have to spend on sick-kid groceries). It felt as though we were both doing a good deed, and I know for sure that Sean has taken it very much to heart, delivering delicious meals and good cheer to sick people he suspects might not have other assistance on days of Dreaded Lurgy.

My all-time very favourite story about this, however, involves me doing almost nothing. A friend named Morgen, not a close one but someone I've known and liked a good while, was on a long celebratory road-trip with his giant dog in his mother's car, when some important system of the car went awry—stranding him and the dog in a small town in New Brunswick, Canada. He posted to Facebook, looking for anywhere he and his giant dog could pitch their tent and use a washroom for free until the car could be fixed—he was too broke to get a hotel room and too trans to use a hostel or a temporary shelter. As it happens, I know someone with ties in rural New Brunswick: a lovely librarian from Nova Scotia I met by accident and got to be friends with after she wrote to ask me some questions about her (then just coming out) trans son. I emailed Marian with Morgen's predicament and—exactly as I'd hoped—she knew someone with plenty of land and a workshop washroom that she was willing to let Morgen use on Marian's say-so, which was really my say-so. He was safe and comfortable until the car was ready and repaired Marian's friend's back steps as well while he was there. And all manner of things were well.

Besides all that, let me just be honest—I have felt so very well cared for by the greater worldwide network of homos, bifolk, and transpeeps, ever since I came out and started going places and doing things. What I've come to realize is that within the larger world, running under the skin of it and beyond notice, are any number of compensatory systems designed to mitigate the effects of discrimination, if not a patch on the hugeness of privilege; they balance the many ways that people can be disempowered or disenfranchised by race or class or religion or gender or ability or sexual orientation. It's a way of saying, and then demonstrating, that we recognize where the larger-world system offers less to people who are not straight, white, middle-class, Christian, and living in unimpaired bodies—and so, in order to make up the difference in our small ways, in these personal transactions and interactions, we'll offer a little more. A little more welcome or a little more wine, a bed or a couch or a ride—some way of extending a small-p privilege to someone who might otherwise not be so well done by.

People have gone way out of their way for me, housed me and fed me, networked for me, hired me, recommended me, passed along their job recommendations and their secret ingredients and their outgrown formal wear and the phone numbers of their favourite tricks. It's rare that I do not feel showered with gifts from the queer-and/or-trans-verse, and so I take my part in this cycle of generosity and caring for my sort of people quite seriously. I *do* look to see who seems like they could stand some extra help. I *am* often trying to problem-solve logistical issues and information requests. Even if I were not generally a helper by both nature and nurture, it seems ... well? Only fair.

When Helga's email came back to me, so full of indignation and unpleasantness, it felt as it was meant—like a rebuke, a slap in the face. She hadn't seen my email as an invitation into the carefully networked balancing force of outcast lovingkindness. She'd only seen imposition in the words. *How dare I?* she was saying, and it was clear from the force of her words that she meant it rhetorically. But, there was a real answer to the question. I dared because so many other people also had and were and would again, made space for me and others, made time for us, made us dinners or appointments or extra drinks. I guess if you live in the arid desert of tribelessness, where there's no oasis but the one you've paid cash for when you're out of your comfort zone, it might be quite a shock to discover in your email someone you faintly know trying to offer your couch to someone you don't know at all. I don't know for sure—between the Jews and the queers and the trans folks I've never had to live that way—but it sounds not unlike Helga: dry and unforgiving. She lives like she expects to always be able to afford to pay, in cash or some other valuable consideration, for whatever she needs. Me, I'd rather share. It's so much nicer this way.

Brother Dog

In a dim bar, in a conspiratorial tone, she asks me: "So? How's butch-on-butch married life?" I shrug and grin, then reply, "I really wouldn't know."

While it's true that my husband, he of song and story and many wonders, is a masculinely gendered person, it is also true that he's not a butch and never has been. I'm not trying to suggest that he's insufficiently handy with tools or excessively interested in his hair or whatever your personal classifiers of butchness are. It's simply true—he is not a transman of butch experience, as some of us are, but rather a faggot of faggot experience, with a side order of homoflexible interest in a certain type of bossy, brash girl (and really, even the six-est on the Kinsey scale could understand that, no?). He has always danced at the boy bars and joined the men's discussion circles, always had a dragwear section of boas and tutus in his closet. He never was a butch. It's simply not his thing.

The butch-on-butch action in my life, instead, is enjoyed with my boyfriend, one of the aforementioned transmen of butch experience and overall a guy so much like me that we refer to each other with great fondness as being of the same breed, like brother dogs. He's the one with the anachronistically formal manners when ladies (self-identified) are present, the one whose nearly stone sexuality was formed at a similar junction of shame and desire; his hands rest on a table exactly the same way mine do. It was a full year of dating before we found any measure of grace on the topic of who would open the door for whom.

Butches, the butches I have known and loved and been protected by, are the ones who find our way through the fire and emerge both singed and hardened, but also smelling of a particular experience that cannot be counterfeited. I find that I recognize the whiff of it across lines of race or class, that butch heart, that big and battered tool of so many unexpected reconciliations, unlikely forgivenesses, full-bore love affairs. I recognize it and love it and I seek it out, because I've learned that it makes my heart melt and my dick hard.

There's a rogues' gallery of them in my secret heart, the butches I have known up close, in their skin, under whose hands I have eventually and gratefully found a sweaty renewal. I still treasure every experience of butch-on-butch intimacy as a rare and precious thing. I remember the chef whose tattoos I licked my way across while she growled my name, and the postman who let me love him so grudgingly and who I always knew would break my heart, and the activist who cried with relief when I took hold of his cock and called it that, right out loud.

I know what kind of trust it takes when we reach out for someone who knows exactly what we've been through and can also see right through our bullshit. There are dodges I would never try with another butch, diversions away from the tender and difficult truth another butch could never sell to me. When my boyfriend and I are together, we have to schedule hours just to sit and talk, so we can say as much as we need to while we have the opportunity. Which is always a great deal. We talk, and talk, and rub away at one another's fire-blackened façades, rough edges grinding rough edges.

Husband and I repair each other and uplift each other and delight each other; bring new wonders into being every day, curl up together every night, cozy warm. Boyfriend is a hot and painful grind that leaves me improved but sometimes hurting—sweet and grateful, but hurting nonetheless, like the three-day burn you carry home from a hot weekend affair. I couldn't live next to it, but I can crave the next searing hit like a drug sometimes.

The butch can be a closed ecosystem if she or he or ze isn't careful. It's tempting to simply batten down the hatches, resist any further incursions and whatever inclusions they may bring. It's why butches can be such sexist asses, and it's why we can be such fiercely loyal friends—whatever gets in gets magnified, built upon, embellished, and emended until it's huge, especially if it's the sort of thing that flourishes in the dark. If we bring in a spore of shame, we can grow a garden of it between our knees and our ears. Letting the light and air in is the only way to prevent it, and letting the light and air in means opening up.

And so I follow my good sense and my stiff dick and I walk right up to the butches that welcome me, with heart in one hand and aforementioned dick in the other. I adore their fur and their ink, their scars and their sore spots; I have learned to treasure bad backs blown out on years of moving other people's stuff and busted-up hockey knees that prevent even the briefest kneeling. I know to turn out the lights. I know how to make wrestling turn into fucking. I know to show hir a good time, to have the kind of safe sex that's not about preventing infection but about preventing dis-ease. Touching her just right, firm enough to make it clear that I'm not doing anyone but myself any kind of a favour here. Murmuring to him in the dark that he's so fucking hot. Letting my sweat drip onto her face as a mark of pride. Letting him want. Letting him need; brutally beautiful and unsustainable, urgently wanted and too difficult to do more than rarely. Closer to never than seldom.

Right now, just now, I am sanding down an old black filing cabinet so my husband can have it in his office, brilliant and functional and fabulous like him. Every touch of the sander makes a fresh spark and a new small patch of gorgeous raw material, and the metaphor is too perfect to ignore. I get better every time I expose myself to another butch in some way. I am *made* better and hope I am making that butch better as well, sparks and all, burning smell and all, hot and bright and just a little bit revealed. Just a little bit of revelation.

Just the Thing

Some of my most beloved chosen family members have only spent any significant amount of time together in my pantry.

From where I sit every morning at breakfast and every night at dinner, I can see Hanne and Bobby shoulder-to-shoulder on top of a Russian Caravan tea canister for her and a vacuum-sealed bag of small-batch blended mint and cardamom tea for him. They're almost snuggled up, which is difficult to imagine in real life but quite satisfying among the dry goods. In my refrigerator, Morgan and Zev, who do not normally spend a lot of time together—though they, at least, have met, and also have a certain tender shopping relationship going involving the regular shipment of a French candy called Carambar anytime he's in France—pass the long days on the same shelf in the form of Morgan's soy milk and Zev's Perrier, which I imagine in my more fanciful moments as kids sitting on a dock, fishing. Not a lot of conversation, but maybe there could be.

Turner lives in the cupboard, among the canned goods; he's the one without a strong attachment to a particular beverage, but he has a last-resort comfort food which sometimes he just cannot do without, and so I keep Heinz Baked Beans, the British kind in the blue label, bought at an import store, in among my more pedestrian blacks and reds. He has been known to draft any kind of baked beans in a pinch, but these are the taste of his childhood, and I keep some for him to show in my guy-love sort of way that

I am prepared to be even the stop of last resort for him. He gets it. Having lived, purposefully, as a placeless person for more than a year, he values the home he has wherever I am, and my willingness to mark that.

More than anything, that's what these food and beverage items are. I am well enough able to go to the store, even at a moment's notice, if I have an incoming houseguest. Transportation or finances would never prevent me from being able to nip out and get a bit of whatever my loved one eats or drinks the day before they arrive. I could easily use, discard, or send them home with the rest of the tea, or what have you, until next time. But I don't. I keep it here.

Part of why I keep it here is the issue of welcome. In some deep-seated, Jewish-mother way—because, whatever my gender is or may yet be, I was raised to be a Jewish mother—keeping what my loved ones like to eat in the house is a way of welcome. It is my way of saying that any of them is welcomed any time, and that I am always ready to receive them. That, in fact, my house is symbolically always ready to receive them. There's no way any of them could come to spend some time without additional provisions being laid in for the lactose-intolerant, the meat-and-potatoes lover, the vegetarian, the citrus-allergic, the carbohydrate-averse, and so on. But there's something for the first moment, which in my typically melodramatic way I always imagine being a crisis, someone washed up on my doorstep in distress. An emergency. If there is no warning, no time to prepare, I can still produce something that I know will be comforting, desirable, and familiar. It is a way of love, however neurotic, and I assume that it is relatively harmless, so I make room.

But also, partly, my reasons are selfish. I am made comfortable and comforted by objects—I like Things. Not for the love of the thing itself, or hardly ever, but for the love of the person with whom I associate it. It is soothing to look up and see the teas plunked quietly together, reminding me of my friends who can so rarely be physically present. Having these things also carries the possibility that if I am sad or scared or missing someone I love, I could eat or drink something that they love, and that way have a moment of communion across the miles.

I am aware that that sounds a little silly. It's my practice, and it even sounds silly to me. Normal human beings keep photos of their loved ones and kiss them before bed, or wear jewellery or possibly tattoos to mark their affections. In the first place, I am too blessedly well loved to wear even one token from each of the people I love dearly; I would be decorated like an alleyway or a Christmas tree. And in the second place, there is something ineluctably comforting to me about an object, something I can hold or use, not just something to look at. I love the food items that live here with me because they have edges and textures and tastes, and if you one day happened to catch me drinking a bitter, dark tea, which I don't really enjoy, you'd understand that I am tasting what Hanne likes, what she tastes, for the want of her.

So, then, a confession. It's worse, this thing of Things, this tenderness for the Stuff, than I have let on. It does not stop at the pantry. These people do not just live with me in my space as foods and beverages, but in every object they have given to me as a gift. I think that, yes, it is probably perfectly normal to stroke with pleasure a small wall-hanging or a recovered chair that she made just for me, with me in mind. Just as it is reasonable to lay a fond hand on the wooden set of drawers an ex-lover built as a birthday gift for me, and likely also fine to pet the carved elephant

Turner brought me back from a trip and hold, fondly, the coins of the country where Zev lives this particular minute, the kind of currency he handles every day. These are things that well people might do, things which are written about, or should be; it is easy to imagine the romantic lead in a movie trailing hir fingers over the figurine that hir long-distance lover presented before moving off to faraway lands, or the vase which was a gift from Great-Aunt Petunia, now sadly deceased. But they do not seem, in the movies I watch anyway, to do this with their underpants.

Not the trailing, I mean, but the fond tactile communication with an absent person through the proxy of an inanimate object. Me, I do. I know which pair of my large collection of notoriously festive striped or polka-dotted underwear was given to me by whom, and I have been known (though, until today, only to myself) to choose in the morning based on whom I want to have close during the day. Ditto my T-shirts, not only the gifts but also the ones I purchased in a particular place or while travelling with a loved one—I keep Turner on my skin when I wear the one we got together in Clinton, Oklahoma, at that truck stop where the young cook told us where the hottest girls in Amarillo went to party, and Bobby is close by when I wear the fire department shirt we shopped for together in a thrift store somewhere outside Pittsburgh, on a weekend visit during which I also made him eat at Primanti Brother's with me twice. In Italian, I have just learned, the phrase for a close friend is *un'amici stretta*, but *stretta* also means a kind of a tight-fitting skirt, and so a close friend is the one you wear tight, close against your body. It seems right.

Company is the word to which I keep returning when I try to explain to more practical people what it is, exactly, that I am doing with all this stuff—why it matters to me whose socks I'm wearing.

I don't need the things to mark the connection in a visible or per-formative way—like an engagement ring or a school sweatshirt. I'm not trying to advertise or signal, and only the officious little wonks in the Stuff and Things Office in my brain know exactly who is being invoked on a given day. No one else can tell (or, probably, would care). But some kind of magic is clearly at work. It's something I can understand as being related to one of my few recurring dreams. In it, I am touching a drop of blood to the hems and cuffs of my loved ones' clothes; patiently going from closet to closet in the night and repeatedly flicking my knife, drawing blood, and making a mark which I understand in the dream is a mark of connection and (by extension) protection. In my dream-scape, just having a bit of me there is somehow a protection to my friends, in much the same way that having a bit of them with me seems like a protection to me.

The want of company, and the protection it brings, extends fur-ther, into my working life. The handkerchiefs I use for blowing my nose are ones that Zev brings me, carried from every warm country to home, but the floral one in my sport-coat pocket was Hanne's. I have stacks of them (I am a handkerchief-carrying kind of a butch), but I carefully re-fold and re-pack that one, because it keeps me from being alone onstage or behind the lectern. Before every talk or performance, I take a moment to effect the sym-bolism of it, my own mini-Shabbos: I remove every workaday thing from my pockets, the money clip and keys and phone and accumulated receipts and change. I put them together in my bag and reverently slide the handkerchief into my pocket. It keeps me company, up there by myself.

It's the blessing and the curse of my travelling-circus life, you see, to meet wonderful people at every stop along the way—and then have to leave them there. In this moment in my life, my closest friends are scattered across North America, most of them a long drive or a short flight away. Even still, for me, it isn't so bad— my peripatetic life allows for arranging gigs in cities where there are people I love, stopping by Pittsburgh or Atlanta on my way home from somewhere else, flying to Barcelona for a weekend. But there's no hope of running into them on the street; most are too far away to call and say, "I miss you, let's have lunch," without it being a flight of fancy or a massive undertaking. The time we get together is planned well in advance and subject to finances and work schedules and so forth even more than usual friendships are—it is mostly not possible to spend ten minutes and collect a hug, or have someone over for a cheap breakfast of eggs and toast. Sometimes because they're far away from my home, and sometimes because I am, but still—not possible. The wonders of the Internet and my unlimited-minute-per-month mobile phone plan notwithstanding, I am often someplace, by myself, wishing for the fond company of the people I enjoy.

This is not, I should say, the voice of complaint. Or, mostly not, anyway. The marvellous, brilliant, fascinating, queer warriors and heroes and storytellers I love so much are scattered all over the world, and if I weren't in a lot of places every year I would never get to meet, much less enjoy, them at all. It seems like a blessing to have a life in which I can meet such rare and wonderful people, rather than relying on my own home city for all my friendship needs. It's just that … well? Sometimes I miss them. I don't mind missing people; I think sometimes that the absences are almost an extra gift because when we see each other again there's so much to talk about and such great joy in it. But I miss them.

And so, I want their company, and I have it how I can—through things. I discovered the trick of this in college, when my beloved great-aunt Flora died, and my grandmother asked me if I wanted the afghan she'd knitted for her sister, which was covering her at the moment of her passing. I was surprised to realize that I really did. I collected it in a shopping bag at her funeral, took it back to school and, after a few days working up to it, curled up under it on my bed to read on one crappy New England fall afternoon. On paper it seemed sort of gruesome—I am using the blanket my great-aunt died under. But in the moment, I also remembered my favourite childhood book, *Good Night, Mr. Tom*, about a refugee child from bomb-blitzed London who goes to live in the country, for safety. Near the end, his best friend Zach is killed while visiting his parents in London, and after some mourning he starts wearing Zach's sweaters and riding his bicycle, as a way to keep him close even after death. It made immediate, intuitive sense to me, even as a child, that one might choose such a thing, and in the matter of Flora's afghan I felt suddenly much warmer, because I was wrapped not only in her blanket, but also in my grandmother's love of her sister.

Preferring not to wait until people are dead these days, I keep the things that belong to or remind me of my loved ones close, visible, present, and feel comforted by them when I do. I like looking around my space and seeing it, all of it: the great large stuffed bear with which my brother Jeffrey gifted me on my sixteenth birthday, the framed vintage photograph Zev found and presented because he knew I would adore it, the four-leaf clovers my beloved Ishai picked for me. But they are no more or less company than the matches I grabbed at the place Abi and I had dinner last, the pair of Turner's dirty socks he left behind crumpled under my bed, or the bottle of artificial tears on my bathroom shelf that Bobby bought here because he'd forgotten his at home and then left in anticipation of future visits. They're all things I smile to see, and if you are imagining me grinning idiotically into space while vaguely pointed in the direction of my laundry basket then you have the right idea here. I can't help it. I like The Stuff.

Because of this, because in my monkey mind everything works the same for everyone else as it does for me, I also want all of my friends and loved ones to keep objects of me close by, for similar purposes. I understand, rationally, that not everyone has the sheer sappiness to feel comforted by a pair of my dirty socks, and I am completely prepared to accept that my cast-off toiletry items, left-over beverages, and assorted matchbooks are probably not treasured by my friends because they are mostly less mentally ill than I am, or at least differently so. This, I am forced to conclude, is a good thing. And because of this, I not only bring them things but also send them things in the mail, things chosen for them, things I imagine they might enjoy using or having. That way, I imagine, we can all quietly keep each other company without anyone being forced into a more intimate relationship with dirty laundry than ze is ready for.

It turns out that this is a partially effective strategy. Visiting Turner, I was struck and delighted by all the places where I exist in his space. Postcards stuck up on the walls, souvenirs of our trips together, photos of us. The gifts I brought him were immediately installed on the mantel, where I imagine they remain. A peripatetic performer like me, Turner furnished his entire apartment in things collected while travelling and things given to him by his friends, a sort of a super-concentrated Home Experience for someone who isn't home much, as I used to not be. I get it.

But many of the other people in my life, as much as they love me, turn out to only need so many bookmarks (which is the true purpose of the postcard, in case you had not been aware). They grin at the funny-looking candy bars I send, eat them, discard the wrappers, and go on with their days. They very helpfully mail me back whatever I left behind unless I am explicit that I have left it on purpose, in which case they are mostly a little puzzled (though occasionally delighted). These are people who seem to believe that it is possible to keep someone close in your life without making a fetish of the crappy plastic keychains you both got at Rehoboth Beach.

Me and my monkey brain, we both know it is possible, and in my rational mind I do not blame anyone for this. It seems sensible and healthy and also very tidy. My heart, however, tells a different story. It leaps when I'm at a friend's house and see a letter I sent months ago lying on an end-table, and it sinks when I don't see any of the things I have carefully chosen and sent anywhere around. I can't help myself. Stern talkings-to from the logical lobe of my brain have not always dismissed this sense of lack perceived by my tender heart, which wants to be wanted as company in a way it can recognize and understand.

The introduction of Bobby into my life, a person who has very strict personal rules about the accumulation of stuff, is helping matters on this front. Early on, I sent a pair of pyjama trousers, the kind of cheap cotton knockaround pants everyone has for in the morning before it's time to put on the armour and go out into the world. I thought they would suit him, and I was pleased to imagine pants I had sent against his skin, which I was missing the day I sent them. But it turned out he already had a pair of pyjama pants, and a firm policy abut getting rid of one item of clothing for every new one he brought home. I had broken the rules—about which he was extremely gracious—but he reiterated them very clearly, if very kindly. Please not to be sending anything which could not be either consumed or discarded when he was finished with it. Thank you.

(This was not the first time this had come up. Here I offer my sincerest apologies to everyone I have ever loved who has found hirself holding some piece of nonsense I'd sent with all good intentions but no discernible sense. Sorry about that. In case you still have a stash of crap from me in the back of a drawer somewhere, I now officially encourage you to throw it out or pass it on.)

And yet, even still, it is clear that the now-owner of the pants loves me—he kept the pants out of the fond, stupid love of me—and wants my company. He, however, seeks it in his own way, not mine. And perhaps as that conversation took place, and his clear explanation sunk in, I started to be willing for the first time to believe that a thing of mine, or things I sent, was not the only way to have my company. Certainly I believed this in theory. But somehow, the empathy-meter clicked over and the little light came on. I get it now. Turns out you can teach a monkey brain a thing or two.

That all said—it does not stop *me*. I am almost completely comfortable with the idea that other people do not have the same relationship to Things as I do, and I do not feel bad, now, to know that someone has examined the bit or bob I have sent them from Honolulu or Pittsburgh and smiled and then recycled it. It's enough, the smile is enough. But for myself, I am resigned to a long life of carefully curating the objects in my view, or in my day, and looking at them as though they were the sleeping forms of my loved ones, even though they would probably not sleep together in such a fashion. I still fondle things, like a clothespin or a bottle-cap, which look like so much trash but call up profound sense memories all afresh for me. I will continue, impervious to reason or good sense, to grin fondly at other people's dirty laundry, and Hanne and Bobby will remain tucked up together in the pantry, quietly, aromatically, reminding me that I'm loved.

The Intimacy of the Pack

For Ushi, 2002–2013

When I woke up on the morning I understood that this story was a story, only the left side of me was cold. I sleep, habitually, on my belly, curled slightly inward to my belly-down left, and that's the cold side. On my right I was warm, because Pax was pressed against me from armpit to knee; his breathing even and his whiskers only slightly tickly against the sensitive skin of my bare side. Without really thinking about it, I shifted slightly back toward him for more warmth and contact, which he accepted with a small sigh, and I drifted back off to sleep.

It's a tender scene, the kind of sleep-time intimacy anyone might have at home with his dog, but that was neither my bed nor my dog; they were my lover's, and I was a guest. He had four dogs, and they—over time, and with a certain investment on my part of head-scritching, treat-dispensing, early morning walking, covert scrap-dropping, and even occasional lap-sitting—decided that I was a part of their pack. They were so clear in this regard that those dogs who would rush pell-mell to the window and bark if a very large acorn fell from a tree would allow me to drive up, park, and walk right into the bedroom where their human was asleep without more than a scuffling, whuffly greeting at the door when I arrived.

In return, I learned not only their names but their habits and preferences and histories. Old Gus got the spoon to lick if anything good was being prepared and always got in the car first on adventure mornings; Hawley firmly believed himself to be a lapdog (all eighty-five pounds of him) but hated to have his paws touched and it took two people, several Twizzlers, and a lot of patience to clip his toenails. Irene wanted to be scratched just above her tail, hard, none of that namby-pamby stuff, and had to have her toy before she headed out for a walk. Pax, my most frequent heating pad, liked to supervise all human trips to the bathroom and was head-shy until he knew me very well. They all knew that I tended to sit backward in a kitchen chair when I was only feeling up to scritches but would allow all polite comers when I was on the sofa, and they knew that my appearance often meant meals getting cooked as opposed to heated in the microwave (which meant pots and pans to be licked clean). They knew their human loved me. We were all pals.

The process of getting to know someone's companion animals is a kind of intimacy I have always treasured especially. My childhood best friend Rachael lived with two beagles, Bagel and Bialy, and I loved feeling safe—including within my socially anxious self—during parties and group play dates when Bagel, slightly skittish around packs of six-year-old girls, would come sit close to me and lick my dirty feet. I wanted a dog desperately as a kid, but my mother (fairly, I have to say) felt that two children under five were more than enough work and that since I could go pester Rachael's beleaguered beagles whenever I cared to, my dog-related needs were probably well enough met, for the moment.

In high school, my closest friend Lisa had a brace of Maltese, and after a while they raced to the front door at the sound of my voice (well, they raced to the source of any noise, but after a while I got to tell the difference between the "Hey, what's that?" behaviour and the "Hooray! Look who it is!" behaviour). Dancing around my feet on their stubby little hind legs, they'd sing their funny little Maltese song of a bark—a noise so distinctive that Lisa and her folks and brother could all mimic it to call the dogs and also used it in crowded spaces to echo-locate one another. At first I was nervous that I'd step on one of them, and it took me a whole year of rather frequent visiting to be able to tell them apart, but eventually I knew Pepper and Callie and Nikki and Niblets on sight, and in the fullness of time was amazed that anyone ever confused them. Niblets, who we joked was a lesbian due to her absolute refusal to breed with—or even go near—a male dog, was my particular friend. We spent countless hours snuggled together into the deep cushions of the purple living room couch, watching movies and sharing bowls of popcorn next to Lisa and Pepper, who sat roughly the same way.

Then for a while I had my own dog, a beautiful and perfect mutt of a dog named Ulric who slept curled up by my calf or next to my head depending on some algorithm I was not privy to, and who had countless quirks and postures that were immediately discernible to me but which other people couldn't necessarily interpret. These minute distinctions are the result of living cheek by jowl with someone all the time. In the same way I knew my ex-wife Nicole's level of interest in what someone was saying by the shape her mouth made as she listened, I knew how Ulric felt about a new noise by the angle at which he tilted his head at the source of it.

It's the belonging that's really at the heart of my pleasure in getting to know someone's animals. It speaks of such a particular kind of intimacy; it means that not only is this someone you know well, but that this is a house you visit. Not just to pick someone up, but for long talks or overnights or leisurely dinners or some other suitable piece of time during which an animal could get used to your presence. It means that you have had the time to be here, to be present and attentive to the place and its inhabitants. It is, I think, a cousin of the point at which you suddenly realize that you know where everything is kept in the kitchen—a sense of being a part of the life of that place, that family, those people, in a way that no declaration ever could no matter how lovingly created it might be. I could write any number of fond things about the presence of Zev in my life, but the most specific and telling thing I can imagine saying about how completely he is part of my family and my heart is that my dog will poop for him without hesitation.

Similarly, that lover and I—who never managed to actually have a conversation about what we are to one another that I am able to recall—both found it inordinately comforting and quite significant that his eldest gentleman dog Gus, the standoffish curmudgeon, eventually began to come and present his head to me for petting from time to time. Neither of us wore any kind of love token from the other (nor were we even particularly in the habit of introducing the other as "my lover"; I only use it in this essay to explain why I was spending so much of my time sleeping in his bed). They all seemed sort of superfluous in the face of old Gus, a doddering, rheumy, arthritic fourteen-year-old, dipping his head with great gravity to accept my attention. It makes our limited range of human ways to claim a person as part of one's pack seem a little ridiculous.

There is, it must be said, a performative aspect to this as well. I continually encounter people invested in being "dog people";

strangers who ask my own dog's name and then attempt to call or instruct her, believing that she'll obey them. She'll sit, especially if they're holding something that looks likely to be a snack, but mostly she is focused on me and how I'm reacting to them. Whatever drives the human urge to be someone whom dogs (and, I notice, children) will respect and obey, its flipside is that we are pleased and proud when an animal (or a child) chooses to connect with us to the point where he or she will voluntarily take instruction or direction from us. It is clearly a sufferance of fondness, and it is one which we humans find deeply gratifying.

I'm absolutely guilty of being proud of it, and what's more— guilty of showing it off. At a party some years ago for my treasured friend Hanne, I sat in her packed living room with a variety of people who were all cooing at her Japanese Akita, Ushi, a deliberate and dignified dog with excellent manners and a certain distrust of strangers. Somehow, this devolved into some of the partygoers calling him to see if he would come and be loved on. An assortment of kissy-noises, thigh-pats, whistles, and snaps were brought to bear in the attempt, but when there was a moment of quiet I said, "Ushi, come," into it, just as his people say it, and he unhesitatingly came and looked up into my face as if to say, "How can I help you?" There was an admiring murmur in the room, and I scritched him under his chin just where I know he likes it as a reward for making me look good.

Ushi, like most dogs, is smart—he must have known that all of those people saying his name wanted his attention, or wanted him to come to them. For whatever reason, he honoured my request. Maybe because he knew for certain that I know where he likes to be scritched and would give him the most pleasant reward. Maybe as a way to mark me as a member of his family, maybe because mine was the instruction he is conditioned to reflexively obey. Maybe on a whim. But the ineffable sense of belonging in that moment and all the ones like it—when Bialy was eventually willing to walk on a leash with me, when Niblets started to seek me out when I stayed over and sleep in the inside curve of my knee, when Ushi started sitting down on my feet from time to time, even when Irene started dropping her bone on my head in the morning to announce her desire to have breakfast, please—those moments of belonging can't be faked.

There's nothing insincere in a dog, nothing dishonest, and yet they are so attentive to the people in their lives. Being welcomed by someone's dog is an unmistakable and also an unassailable sign of intimate connection. My dog knows exactly how I feel about the various people who visit my house and treats them accordingly; she also follows my example. So when I arrive at the door and I am greeted fondly by the people and dogs, it settles even my famously insecure emotions—I am no longer afraid, at least for the moment, that this person I like so well is merely humouring me. Her dogs have expressed the mood of the pack, and as dogs cannot dissemble the reassurance is beyond argument or reproach.

As I write this, my good dog Levi Jane is asleep on the sofa next to me, her head resting on my thigh in one of those positions that looks like a chiropractic nightmare to human eyes but is evidently very comfortable if you're a dog. It is one of her most familiar, most intimate behaviours and one of the kinds of closeness I cherish most, writing sprawled out in my own un-ergonomic way on the couch with Levi Jane tickling my knee with her old-lady dog breath, occasionally opening an eye to check my progress, probably wondering when she'll get the last walk of the day before going to bed. Her little ways are as familiar to me as my own voice, by now, and the only other person who knows them like I do is my husband Ishai, whose dog she was first. He's had other partners in their thirteen years together, and she had been introduced to all type and manner of people before I came into the picture, but he says I am the only one she ever treated like her person.

(If you were convinced that I have always been a lovely person with an unblemished heart, you should know this: it's a source of considerable satisfaction to me that Levi Jane used to piss all over the belongings of Ishai's ex—the one who was so unkind to me for so long—when they lived together. When he revealed that she once savaged a treasured first edition belonging to said ex, I could not help myself; I felt glad. Now you know.)

These days, I know all the things required to care for Levi Jane, her little habits and ways. I can help my friends or lovers do their doggy tasks, but only with an instructional narrative and a certain amount of patience on everyone's part, including the dogs. My sailing friends joke that the only instructions you can give a novice sailor are "Pull that thing!" and "No, the *other* thing!" until one day suddenly no words at all are needed. It seems the same with dogs. I found myself once on a Sunday morning at that former lover's house while we were still in the thick of the affair, stumbling toward the door during dog-walk prep at some ungodly hour of the morning, absently picking up Irene's toy and handing it to her because I know that if she doesn't have a toy in her mouth during the mad rush to the car, she might nip one of her brothers; later I saw said lover put his finger on the button to lower the back windows and then cast a curious glance into the backseat. I nodded, knowing that he wanted to know if Irene had put the toy down yet and would therefore not be likely to drop it out the window—I could see that she had. With the window down, we shivered a little while not talking at all, and the moment passed. I didn't even notice what had happened until I fished the toy out of the car later.

I've just made a new friend who has dog, a dog I haven't met, and when he sent me a photo of himself, it showed him in his front yard, holding his handsome girl Magna, a grand dame of a Rottweiler. It makes me like him better that he sent a photo that included his dog, and as I look forward to getting to know him I am also looking forward to getting to know her, and liking her, too. It seems like a lovely prospect, to become a part of this man's life in a way that might allow me some intimacy with his dog as well. I have discovered that now, with Levi Jane in my life, I am gladder when my new friends have dogs or want them, and that thinking about dog walking together is always a good sign. It seems, in the end, somewhat easier to learn about a person with a dog, and also easier to like him. Also, easier to know if I am liked in return. I just have to ask the dog.

Diesel Femme

I've fallen for girls like you a hundred times, you foul-mouthed and fresh-faced girls with the biggest smiles and the roughest hands and the softest bellies. There's something about it, something about the hearty blend—it makes even the starchiest boys a little bendy (and, honestly, even the bendiest boys a little stiffer, if you know what I mean, and I think that you do). So when those shade queens in their tasteful ensembles look at you sideways or cut-eyed because your fingernails are filed short, or because you sometimes might say "ain't" in the same sentence as "heteronormative," or because you still have derby bruises or rock-gym scrapes, please remember, diesel femme girl, we need you. You are a brave and special thing.

And please, do not listen to anyone who says stupidly, out of hir ass or other darkened orifice, that you're some kind of a butch in femme clothing, or even worse—I'm almost afraid to say it, in case you've been spared this particular idiocy, but—do not listen when anyone says you're not really a femme. That's sexism talking, pure and simple. That faint faraway rumble you hear in the background of such a pronouncement is a thousand years of powerful women spinning in their graves, and the last fifty years worth revving up their power tools because, really? Butches—any butch even remotely worth the appellation—we know about femme power. And we love it.

Admittedly, some of us like it in different ways, in a variety of flavours, just like some femmes love a dandy butch (thank goodness) and some prefer to welcome the rough-and-tumble kind. No matter. Likewise, some butches are comforted by the women who will tend and heal us after a battle of some kind, and some of us lose our hearts to the kind of girl who will stand and fight in her heels, right alongside.

Me, I have always tended a little altar to the diesel femmes and even these days, all gayed up with my handsome husband and my very own six-foot pink feather boa, I still sit up straight for the women who call that out in me. Not just the ones I've enjoyed in the horizontal way, either (though I still think about that chef, the one who was decorated in nicks and burns who bossed me the whole time we were fucking and then pulled me up over her like so many blankets, and snuggled down, and fell fast asleep), but both the girl I've loved for twenty years and kissed twice, once per decade, and the woman with whom I made the very sensible decision not to pursue an affair but still have the occasional clutch about. Especially in sundress weather, when her shoulders are bare.

It must be said that they do not have a lot in common, on the surface. Nevertheless, there I have been, year upon year, sitting with them, being my shiniest while trying not to stammer with the heat of them so close. Not ever both of them at the same time, which I am not sure I could stand. It would be too much like climbing into the burning woodstove and closing the door behind me. Though, oh, what a way to go.

Maybe it's because I like a little bit of gender-bending, or a lot of it. Maybe because I think competence is sexy. Maybe just because of the way they talk to me, girls like you all, teasing me and instructing me with great good humour and perfect confidence. I know it's not real perfect confidence, not always; I know that you suffer, breathless and gasping, in the trough of insecurity between waves of mastery. I know you take days off from lipstick. I also know you feel the weight of your "Fuck you, I got this" persona sometimes, and I live humbled and privileged in the days that you've called me from there. Sometimes I can come and sit quietly, massaging or chauffeuring you while you hand me the whole business to hold for a minute so you can straighten up and stretch. Other times my job is to come and be your foil, to compose myself into an attentive good dog straining slightly at his leash, so you can find your way back into your eyebrows and hosiery.

It has been my honour, each time. I understand some of what trust and vulnerability means for the diesel femme, the stone grrl, and I hold it in the same silk-cushioned room of my heart in which I keep every other artifact of power laying itself down to my witness in whatever way. And when I need a rest, I know I don't even have to ask you, you're so sweet to me—you'll boss me into a break, leaving me no choice but to rest. I love you for that.

I love all the ways you see me, fierce girl—for the way you lick your lips and grin when I arrive in an outfit meant to please you, whether it's a dinner jacket or cut-offs, and for the way you're the first one to catch the stumble in my sentences and suggest that this is the last question of the evening. I love the way you know how soft-hearted I am and like me anyway. I love you for how brilliantly you can make me feel big without ever making yourself small. And I love you maybe most of all for all the ways you try to fix it for me, all the while pretending that's the furthest thing from your mind—the bumps you try to smooth, the curious stares you try to steer me away from, the gossip you try to keep from ever reaching my ears, the meannesses you can somehow take the bite out of right away with your hand on the back of my neck. You claim me, for just a minute, and I remember.

I remember how much we're partners in this deal. I remember that being a dandy butch faggot fella such as I am, I might seem like the opposite of you, but I'm not—I'm the reverse. We're the negative image of each other, maybe, but in the same photo. The picture is the same. We're outliers, I guess, or outlaws or something, but I see how we keep the traction up for two decades and I think, you know what? Sometimes it might be true that the best partner for a hurricane is a well. But sometimes, the best partner for a hurricane is another hurricane, if they can get more or less synced up to spin. You never blamed me for choosing a tender-hearted farmboy who matches his cute underpants to his cute striped socks, just like I have never blamed you when the butch you take up with for a minute or forever is the kind with a factory-installed dick. These things happen. We each need someone who's up to us. Our kind of hurricanes can be hard to find.

I dearly hope to spend the rest of my life getting beard burn and sharing buttondowns with my husband, this is true. We do that sometimes, my kind and your kind both, and we don't hold it against one another because how do you fault love, even stupid love? But please let there be no mistake: I do see you. I see you, and I know perfectly well that people who pretend not to recognize you are lying because they're scared of how powerful you are. Pay no attention to this, please, if only for my sake. Please don't get discouraged. Please do not stop your shining. I probably could live in a world where no brilliant bruised-up grown woman in proper stockings ever again raised an eyebrow at me and made me flush red from neck to knee.

But, girl, I think you know—I wouldn't want to.

Gathering Light
Out of Darkness

Imagine it.

Imagine it's dark, and things are uncertain, and you're afraid.

Whether it's 2,200 years ago or yesterday, there is only one thing that you want—only one thing that you need—and it's light. It's not an accident that Chanukah is a holiday that we observe with light, it's not an accident that so many religious holidays, especially the ones in the deepening dark of winter, are commemorated with light. It's not an accident that the *ner tamid*—the eternal flame that hangs in every synagogue, the one thing every synagogue must have—is the light. A light that never goes out; a light to help us find our way.

The story of Chanukah is simple on the face of it: a small band of Jews, as is so often the case in these Jewish military victory stories, through wit, divine intervention, guile, or pure good luck, succeed over an enemy. In this case it's the Seleucid Empire, though frankly this story is pretty portable through history and it could just as well be King Ahasuerus or Pope Gregory VII, which at least I can pronounce. In this case, the revolt was against King Antiochus IV, who pillaged and looted the Great Temple—more or less outlawing Judaism by destroying the seat of it—and turned it into an altar to Zeus. At which pigs were sacrificed, for the extra sacrilegious icing on the already brutal cake. This sparked a revolt, and the revolt of the Jews against the Hellenizers was successful. At the end of their labours of battle, the victorious soldiers returned to the temple, the seat of their religious and legal lives, to put to rights what the invaders had destroyed and re-light the *ner tamid*, the eternal light, making it again bright, making it again holy.

But when they went to do this, they found that the olive oil reserved for that lamp—specially pressed, sealed, and sanctified—had been desecrated. It took seven days then, at that time, to press and consecrate jars of oil to light the *ner tamid*. One jar per night, and there was only one uncorrupted jar remaining. In my mind's eye I see it rolled under a curtain-end or behind a bookshelf, unnoticed by the invaders but precious to the returning Jews, triumphantly re-taking possession of the Temple. I imagine it happening in the rush of adrenaline after the fight, on the collective high of good news, people streaming in with their buckets and brushes and tools to make the Temple ready before Shabbat— mourning the loss of so many things and then rejoicing in the dim building to have found one jar of oil after all. Lighting it in full recognition that it wouldn't last long enough, but joyous: so joyous to have the means to make things right again after so long, and to know that the light would burn as a bright Fuck You to the retreating remnants of the Greek army; that the glow would dog those tired, defeated marchers all the way back to their ruler. We're back, it would say, and we are not afraid of you—even wounded, even in mourning, even with loved ones captured or their whereabouts unknown. Even if all we can get out of this jar is one night's light, we're not afraid, and we're not waiting anymore.

Brightness. Resistance. Mourning shot all through with black-eyed, bloody joy. And the Talmud, which says comparatively little about Chanukah and its observance, is specific about one point—your menorah, your lights of Chanukah, should be displayed outside your door or in your window, on the side opposite the *mezuzah*; it should be visible to the street, it should say, "Here we are. Here we are, and here is our brightness."

Except, as the text notes, in times of danger. The written work that was collected as the Talmud was opened just a few hundred years after the final destruction of that Great Temple. "Times of Danger" was not a theoretical concept.

Some years there's a long break, even as much as a month, between Transgender Day of Remembrance and Chanukah. The long break has always been a long enough period to let me forget Trans Day of Remembrance by the time Chanukah rolls around; by then I am busy trying to finish my holiday shopping and get to all the things I have been invited to roughly on time and carrying the correct thing—scent-free host gift, appetizer since my surname begins with a B, allergy meds in case these hosts have cats—we've been to their house ten times but neither of us can remember. That's what takes up my time. Gift wrap and cat dander. Trans Day of Remembrance is forgotten.

Trans Day of Remembrance, like Kwanzaa, is often derided as a "made-up holiday," as though other holidays have existed since the dawn of time, as though dinosaurs strung cranberry garlands and "Kiss Me I'm Irish" T-shirts gained popularity during the Cretaceous period. It's the day we gather to remember our dead—those trans people, mostly transwomen, mostly women of colour—who have been murdered in the previous year for the grave and terrible crime of being transsexual or transgender. Evidently, it does not matter how marginalized a group is, there's always some extra room to shit on women and people of colour.

Let it not be said that the haters are slacking. They know who they can best get away with targeting.

The first vigil came two weeks after Rita Hester was murdered in Boston. Hundreds of people poured into the streets in outrage when the details were released—she had been stabbed more than twenty times, and left for dead. A robbery gone bad. Probably, the police said, the work of a john. That Rita was never a sex worker made as much difference to their conclusions as the fact that anything a robber would have taken was still in her apartment, covered in her blood.

Her people lit candles and they marched. They walked down the Allston, Massachusetts street from the bar where she was last seen alive to her apartment and they stood in a bright cluster under what had been her window, first chanting and then singing. Their display was unmistakable, their sorrow as huge as their resistance—here we are, they chanted, here we are. Here we are, Rita, come to soothe your restless ghost and pray you home to wherever your G-d is, so you can sit by her right hand and rest yourself a while. Here we are, you attackers, you cowards, come now and bring your knives, and let us just see whether you can stand the heat of all these flames. Let us see whether you could even extinguish one of them. Here we are, Boston Police, and there are more of us where this came from, and we are not going to stop calling and writing and pestering you for answers and behaving as though we are entitled to them, which we are.

Every year there are more candles to light as the annual count grows. I want to love any increase of brightness, but lighting a candle for every murdered transperson in the past year is not one of those times. I wish the number of flames would dwindle. I am in that moment of the House of Shammai, he who argued that

Chanukah candles should start at eight and dwindle down to one. Hillel's method, the increase of light, was adopted instead, and it seems correct to me even when I separate it from "tradition," also known as, "the way we've always done it in my family ever since we started having the holiday at our house instead of Bubbe Rachel's." Light should increase in times of joy; in times of sorrow, light should increase. I do not think these are contradictory positions.

We should mourn. We should notice the qualities of defeat. We should stand out in the cold wind and say the names of our dead out loud, *l'shem shamayim*, for the sake of heaven and after this is done, after each of their names has burned in our mouths and we have tasted the bitter soot of sorrow, then we should light our candles and we should be there. We should say, we are here. We should, in sorrow and in resistance, increase the light. When the heart is dark, when the mood is dark, all we want is a little sanctified light. We want it to sputter and catch, and lift our hearts up as it does.

In the story of Chanukah, we're brought over and over again to the understanding that the miracle of this jar of oil is only on the surface the fact that it burned longer than anyone expected that much oil to burn. That's kind of cool, but we don't make it a holiday. What happened in the Temple 2,200 years ago is that the hearts of Jews—miserable in defeat, locked away from their source of religious observance—were in darkness. They were in despair. And when the light came back on, when they saw the international, wordless, perfect symbol of We Are Here, they rejoiced in it.

I hope that someday transpeople too have the occasion to call light out of darkness, that we too can celebrate our resistance with friends and family. I would enjoy it very much. But until then, we are going to have to resist, and we are going to have to get better and smarter and more cohesive and more compassionate and more resolute in our resistance. That is the light that we can call out of this darkness. We are the light that we can call out of this darkness.

And make no mistake, it will require all the qualities of a candle. It will require us to make ourselves visible, eye-catching even, when we might rather hide. As long as we think we can stay safe, we will have to do it, and we will have to pay attention to how "safety" works and who gets it and why. We will need the candle's brightness, especially when things are dark—metaphorically dark, I mean, when the next report of the next murder is announced we will have to let go of muttering "such a shame" and instead celebrate what would have been her birthday with a giant cake that has her right fucking name on it and deliver slices to the police station and the newspaper. We may indeed need to burn, to allow ourselves to be a little consumed by our resistance, to give something of ourselves to the fight and assume that it may not be returned, that what we sacrifice will become worthwhile in the fullness of time but is unlikely to be returned to us personally. On the other hand, resistance fighters are well-known to be smarter and sneakier and more nimble and better-looking than the soldiers of armies; resistance values the trickster above the blunt follower of orders.

Look for it in the wintertime, if you want to find The Light Of The Season—the real light, not the Hallmark one. Look for the location of resistance. Look for the darkness in which you can be a spark. Look for the opportunity to be bright, to light someone else's way, to warm their hands, to shuttle them safely through the dark. Look for the crack you can fill or the shadow you can dispel by bringing a little bit of the light of resistance, carefully and precisely, to just the place where it is needed. Look for the place of being bright—of being bright and present outside your own house, or in the window, on the opposite side to the *mezuzah*, letting anyone who passes know.

We are here.

When I Am Old
and Grey and Full of Sleep

I am old enough, now—nearing forty, knees starting to go, and so on—that I wonder about my old age. I assume I'll have one; I come from a luxuriously long-lived family. With just the one exception, all of my grandparents and great-aunts and uncles have lived into their late eighties or early nineties. Of the ones who have lost their marbles none have done so until eighty-five at the earliest (my Nana, my mother's mother, is eighty-nine and has not only all her own marbles but those belonging to several other people, which we're fairly certain she won while trouncing them at bridge). It seems reasonable to assume that I will have an old age to enjoy, barring (as ever) the unforeseen, and so I wonder about it—what it will look like, whether it will resemble the old ages I have witnessed in my lifetime, if I will be looked after when the time comes, and by whom. Whether I will get to grow old with my beloved partner and my friends like my grandparents did, changing their neighbourhoods from Queens and New Bedford to Fort Lauderdale and Boca Raton, respectively; when my father's parents bought a house in Florida, it was next door to the home of their lifelong best friends, the Temlocks.

I dream of this, wistfully. When we've all outlived our usefulness (and some of us our decorativeness as well), I would love to be on the same street as my friends, somewhere not too cold, playing cards and having lunch dates. I would like to join a book club and a bowling league populated largely by friends and their friends, spoil each other's grandchildren rotten, and make lots of plans to have cocktails and a snack, sit outside and compare medications, and complain about our children who never call. It seems unlikely, but I would enjoy it a great deal—so much that sometimes I look at undeveloped pieces of land or big properties with just a small house on them in the Carolinas, or sometimes Costa Rica. Maybe, I think, if we bought a piece of land now we could all build on it over time, a slow-growing unrepentantly communal retirement community for aged activists. With a little guest quarters for the various children and stepchildren and one day, G-d willing, the grandchildren Stanley will give me and Ishai, with a wee pond and a big garden and a chicken coop because a certain handsome farmboy will give me no peace until he can keep a little flock of chickens, and at that point, why not?

I am looking forward to the age of why not. This age right here does not provide so many moments in which I am free of care.

I wonder, when I think about aging, about what ties will last and which will ravel away or break under the weight of distance or death. Some of my very favourite people are much older and some are unwell, and some are both—when I was twenty and precocious and not afraid of anything, I made some wonderful friends who were quite a bit older than me and now the cold thread of cancer is starting to creep into the conversation, brittle and unwanted. I do not feel old enough to be having serious conversations about whose literary executor I will be and for whose things I will find myself responsible when the time comes—not when these conversations feel immediately relevant and somewhat pressing, I don't. And yet, when I was a sunny youth, I imagined that I would be to them what a child would be; full of idealism and free time. It seemed like we were forging a new kind of family, a queer version, in which we could and would bind ourselves together regardless of blood or marriage. An army of lovers, we said, and anyway hadn't we loved each other better than our families of origin had done? Hadn't we cared for each other more kindly? So, of course, When The Time Came—that's how we put it, capital letters always quite present—When The Time Came, we would be there for each other. I would be there.

This is not entirely how it has worked out. Now I'm not surprised, but then, if someone had told me, I would have been shocked and angry at them for suggesting it. But of the people to whom I was willing to bind myself at age twenty, only one is still in that category. Some of them are not queer anymore, by their own lights—and not because they have chosen opposite-sex partners and had children, but because they have entered themselves into the conclave of the nuclear family, broken it off with their other lovers, erased their pasts. They're now subscribers to the hetero system by which each child cares for her or his parents, or is bad because they haven't. Where you might look in on your former neighbour or old family friend, but no one is going to hold you to that, it's just extra credit work, just karmic gravy. No one would fault you if you didn't. They no longer worry about who will care for them or entertain them or even just keep them company; to whom they will write letters at camp or school or watch as they tear around the place, upending plants. It's not until just now that I am able to see how much of the entire system by which people are able to age either comfortably or miserably depends on our heterosexual-family building blocks. The structure is powerful, in part because it blocks any other methods from view.

Then, too, some of my best beloved and most wonderful friends simply live far away. I don't see them as much as I wish I could now, when I'm healthy and earning money and often on an airplane for one reason or another. I think of them all the time, and we call and we write, but all staying put together is not the same as trying to coax everyone to move somewhere entirely else together, and anyhow—even though they all like one another pretty well at least by virtue of being loved by me—they're not one another's nearest and dearest. They're mine—this isn't like the old neighbourhood, it's the new virtual reality. They all have other, possibly contradictory, needs and obligations and desires. What's more, there's no obligation to square everything or work it out, not really—if we were married, or siblings, we might fight it out until we agreed on Limon or Myrtle Beach or Kitsilano, making tradeoffs about where we'll vacation or how we might fit out a house to encompass this one's dream of a private dock and that one's urgent, lifetime wish for a deep front porch on which to watch the world pass by. But as friends—*just* friends, as the popular construction has it—we might not. We might not even think about it. We will feel glad if serendipity creates something that works, but we won't dig in and fight it out until we're sorted. If I cannot persuade all, or even any, of them to come and retire near to me in thirty years or so, then I'll be with ... whoever else is there, I guess, left to try to make new friends. Why do you think I'm already looking at land, then?

This also makes me wonder—where are the queer elders in my Toronto community? Surely there are, somewhere in this big city, queers who are into their eighties now and would like company, dinner, visitors, and friends. I live right in the gay village; surely they can't be far. Where are they? The ones who are estranged from family, the older folks who are left widowed, the people who are alone and are *feeling* alone? We would be happy to have them over here to eat and have a chat. Some of them are gone to AIDS, never having had the chance to achieve a slightly decrepit old age. But some of them must still be among us.

As it happens, I have partnered and spawned, which gives me some sense of perhaps false security about my golden years. Either my husband or my son could choose to desert me, especially if advanced age makes me more curmudgeonly than I already am, which is very. I hope not; I think I would enjoy being old men together with my sweetheart, and anyhow he promised, after having rushed me into babymaking on the front end of this relationship, that he will live a long, long time so I can enjoy him extra later. Which is one of the sweetnesses of coupledom: a certain amount of freedom from imagining one's self doing laundry for one and cooking a single chop for dinner every night before falling asleep in front of the news, again and again, for decades. Being able to imagine, instead, bickering mildly about whose turn it was to walk the dog and who left their cup of tea on the counter, again; cooking a whole package of spinach or a whole pot of soup. I love the thought of growing old with him whom I have chosen— watching his skin and jaw soften, his teeth go dull, and his laugh lines deepen into canyons. I know I'll be lucky if I get to do this. I know I have been lucky so far.

I had a lover for a while who was seventeen years older and recently separated from his partner while we were involved. He lived in a big house with a huge attic, full of every single thing he'd ever saved, which was a lot of things—box upon box of magazines he thought he might like to read again in the hand-wavy indeterminate future, instructional manuals for electronics long deceased, sometimes in their original boxes right there with the broken equipment. Old telephones and toasters that still partially worked when they were warehoused, in case they might someday be needed again, even though they had been replaced by newer and better-working models. For a portion of the time we were together, the peak of the affair, we used to talk about how all that would someday be mine to sort out—that the house and the dogs and the fourteen years of back issues of *Vanity Fair* would someday all be mine to love or leave. He made me the beneficiary of his work insurance policy in a rash stroke of declaring himself free of his former partner, even though we were not remotely intending a partnership, because he shared my idea that we could make family with whomever we chose. He chose me, and then un-chose me later. To be honest, I assume he also re-assigned his life insurance and the care of his earthly treasures to someone else, but I'm not certain. It's worth mentioning that part of why I'm not sure is that I know he hasn't partnered again. I don't know if he'd bother to change everything, again, until he felt sure of someone the way he once, however briefly, felt sure of me.

My optimistic book title is like my optimistic life, in which I want and believe and hope that I will be able to live and die bound together with my family, my family by blood or marriage or wine or glitter, indiscriminately. But now that I've shed or shirked one whole epoch of my life's worth of friends except the previously mentioned one, I'm afraid that the wine and glitter end up being ... less. I am certainly aware that for them to remain just as binding, I have to walk toward them and work toward them. Where I can turn to my husband and share the details of my day, I have to take two steps more for the non-resident loved ones. Where he and I have to get sorted out before bedtime, I can hold onto more upset than is good for me with someone I'm less entwined with on a daily basis. It means less compromise, and less making up just to go forward, but it also means I have to take the extra steps to move the friendship forward, or it will stagnate and drown. It's more difficult. Sometimes in the dailyness or overwhelm of my partnered, parenting, working life, things get put off a day, or a week. Or longer.

It's true that I get to it, though, even still. That our mail is always more interesting than the neighbours' mail because it's full of parcels and letters and postcards; that my email inbox doesn't just have a Friends folder like I see on other computers, but separate boxes for each of seven different people besides the Friends folder. It's true that they all turned up for my wedding from here, there, and everywhere; that I expect to be at each and every one of their important life events forever. I keep a stash of frequent flyer miles in case of emergency last-minute celebrations or sorrows. I have served all manner of functions for each of them, from the sacred to the extremely profane, and I'm sure there will be more phone calls in the future. I've dedicated this book to them.

I guess we'll see, eventually, as time moves us all forward and I understand myself and my world better. What I am sure for now is that I would like to keep everyone, and that I am willing to keep working to make that happen. Still, again, I hope we can turn to each other. I hope that, whether or not I can find a piece of land I can afford. In my heart, always, we're sloping off into the future, all together.

Please,
Let Me Stay This Lucky

My whole life, I have been inclined to pray. From childhood Shabbos services and Sunday school to right now, I've always felt free to address myself to G-d whenever—sometimes formally and sometimes rather jocularly, in argument and agreement both. I've thanked G-d for bringing me to and delivering me from, for commanding me to kindle and wash and drink, for rainbows and thunder and lightning. When I pass an auto accident, I pray for few injuries and skilled healers to attend the injured; when I hear a fire engine, I pray for a harmless piece of burnt toast. I've experimented with morning and evening prayers, and also with the prayer said after using the bathroom called the *asher yatzar*, which I find incredibly beautiful:

"Blessed is He who has formed man in wisdom and created in him many orifices and many cavities. It is obvious and known before Your throne of glory that if one of them were to be ruptured or one of them blocked, it would be impossible for a man to survive and stand before You. Blessed are You that heals all flesh and does wonders."

For me, G-d is a guiding force. When I pray now, as a grown person, I often pray for help or guidance about a difficult thing or possibly for a good outcome for someone who I love, in love, work, or health. But the prayer I offer most often, more often than any other, is this: please, let me stay lucky.

When I wake up in the morning at home, I come to consciousness quickly so I can silence my alarm and let the little boy sleep a bit longer. He goes to bed in his room, under his night-sky canopy with his fish tank for a night light, but in the middle of the night he comes and climbs in between me and Ishai, usually starfished so he can touch each of us with one hand or foot. I get up a little earlier than he does, so I can go downstairs and start breakfast. Often, before I get up, I push the covers back and give him one little kiss on the sole of each foot; his feet that are still so soft and warm and between you and me I imagine that the kisses travel up through him during the day, with every step, keeping him loved from the inside out. Morgan comes to have breakfast most mornings, since our house is between her house and school and honestly, I think she finds the hubbub energizing, so I go put coffee on and mix pancakes or beat eggs or something, then I go back upstairs to wake Stanley. Ishai comes home from the gym about the same time, so sometimes he and I both get back into bed for a minute and start the day off snuggling the small person awake, singing silly songs to him and holding hands above his head. Stanley, who we joke is on the disco schedule, never wants to wake up, so we play music and turn the light on and talk and kiss him and tug on his big toes until he eventually opens his eyes. When the coffee boils, we spring up to our getting-going stations with a sliver of regret that laying in bed snuggling and singing can't carry on longer. Most days we eat breakfast together, at the table, figuring out the logistics of the day and making our plans for the evening, and when I get up for juice or a spoon I look over and there they all are, shining, sustaining themselves for the day on what I chose and prepared, and I think, please, let me stay this lucky.

Somehow the prayer comes most easily when there's some minor setback or inconvenience—if it rains when I'm walking the dog, when Stanley gets up from the table and is covered in smears of sauce or fruit, when I'm stuck in traffic or at the airport. There's a moment I can feel in the base of my neck, when the tension leeches out and is replaced by the ease of someone who isn't going to snap his pencil and start shouting. That guy, he knows sauce and fruit and rain are temporary and that love endures; he's not worried about getting salsa out of his shirt. I love being that guy—suddenly there's all the room in the world in my head to hear and see what all is happening and think: I can stand and walk. I have a dog and it's safe to walk her where I live. I have this healthy, happy kid and no matter how much food he spills, it won't affect our ability to feed him. I'm in the car or at the airport going somewhere, of my own volition, and once I get there and complete my work or tasks, I can come home again. Home isn't so big but it's safe and comfortable and we can afford it and it's packed with books and plants and art and squashy dinosaurs and there's even room carved out for our guests to be comfortable; I can sit in my big chair and read and write and work and dream. Please, let me stay this lucky.

I know it's not all an accident. I know you have to give love to get love, and I do. I know that, as my Nana is fond of saying, fortune favours the well-prepared. I know I work hard and I know I give and try the best I can. But still, at all sorts of odd moments of the day—when Stanley's jumping on the bed naked and laughing his head off, when I write a sentence that says just what I want it to and nothing I don't, when Ishai's hand finds mine in his sleep, when I reach out for a pep talk or a funny story and my family is there, right there—what springs to my mind and off my tongue before anything else is my little prayer of both request and gratitude.

Please, let me stay this lucky.

S. BEAR BERGMAN is the author of two previous books published by Arsenal Pulp Press: the Lambda Literary Award finalist *The Nearest Exit May Be Behind You* and *Butch Is a Noun*. Bear is also author of two trans-positive children's books, *Backwards Day* and *The Adventures of Tulip, Birthday Wish Fairy* (Flamingo Rampant), and the co-editor (with Kate Bornstein) of the Lambda Award-winning anthology *Gender Outlaws: The Next Generation* (Seal Press). A longtime activist and public speaker, Bear continues to work at the intersection between and among gender, sexuality, and culture. Originally from New England, Bear now lives with his husband and son in Toronto.

sbearbergman.com

Photograph by Zoë Gemelli